The
Fight
for
My Life

My Covid Story

Karen Wasoba

There is no one person I can single
out to thank for this book.

My family and my friends come first
for their tireless work on my behalf.

I also want to thank the doctors and nurses
who used their expertise to preserve my life.

Thanks to those who prayed for me
and helped me through my darkest hours.

I especially thank God,
who not only spared me but is using this miracle
to bring hope and encouragement to others.

I don't deserve all this love, but I am grateful for it.

The names of doctors, medical facilities,
and medications are anonymous to protect privacy.

CONTENTS

1

THE BEGINNING

Something was very wrong. Despite medications, syrups, and an inhaler, I felt like I was trying to bench-press a camel.

Everything felt heavy, and while I wasn't experiencing pain, I was truly suffering. I felt feverish, and my cough was getting worse. Every step was an effort, and I had absolutely no desire to move. It became increasingly difficult to breathe.

It had been four days since I'd returned home to St. Louis after visiting my daughter, Kari, and her husband Gareth in Los Angeles, California; my intention for my trip was to consult with experts at UCLA about a recent concussion, along with prior ones, and see if treatment was needed.

It seemed like a brilliant move; I would go visit family and get some personal business done as well. Kari and Gareth were understandably hesitant about my traveling since the Covid-19 virus was still rampant in the United States and the rest of the world. Kari and Gareth consulted with Ryan and Megan, my son and his wife, and, despite their own misgivings, agreed to let me risk the trip since it was for medical purposes.

Toward that aim, once I arrived, we geared pretty much everything toward my consultation and potential care. Although we did a few small things around town, Kari made it very clear this was a business trip at best. Therefore, there would be no shopping without a mask and no extra bumming around.

Kari

I was nervous about Mom flying, but it had been a long year and we had all been so careful. It seemed justifiable since it was for her wellness, and she would be talking to doctors about possible TBI treatment. It would be a risk, but a calculated one.

I checked with friends who had already been traveling; they assured me that if Mom took precautions, she would be okay. I insisted she double mask and double glove, not eat or drink anything on the plane, and not talk to anyone while in the airport.

Ryan and Megan were not keen about this because they had been very diligent in their own personal protection and felt my flight and exposure to other people was an unnecessary risk. But I think he knew I would probably go whether he agreed to it or not.

Looking back, I realize how reckless I was to assume that I was immune to the virus that was wreaking havoc on the lives of people who were younger and in better physical condition than I was. Maybe I felt that if I didn't think about getting sick, I wouldn't.

After my planned consultation, it was determined that yes, I needed further testing. They wanted to investigate potential damage from past concussions. While I'd hoped they would run the tests immediately, I would have to wait three weeks due to limited availability of the equipment. Kari, Gareth, and I spent some time trying to determine if I should stay with them until then or go home and come back. It would be fun to stay and enjoy the sunshine and the company, but I didn't want to wear out my welcome.

After much discussion, we decided that I would go home and come back later.

Before making the final decision, I noticed that I didn't feel quite right; my ears began to hurt, then my throat felt like I was swallowing razor blades or shards of broken glass. I was unable to sleep because I was so uncomfortable. Then came the feeling of heaviness and not wanting to walk too far or do too much. Everything became an extreme effort.

Instinctively, I knew these symptoms were unusual as I compared them with my prior illnesses. Aches and pains, yes, nausea and coughs, yes. But this pressed-down feeling and near exhaustion was new.

Gareth

Karen stayed with us for ten days, sleeping on a mattress in the living room. I remember she had a cough or sore throat after a few days; Kari and I were a little worried, thinking that it could have been caused by the breeze from open windows or her tendency to snore. We knew she was pretty sick when Karen finally admitted that she felt terrible on the day she was to leave for home.

I tried to act as if everything was fine, but Kari and Gareth weren't fooled. We debated whether I should see a doctor there in LA, but I felt I needed to be treated back home on my own turf if it turned out to be anything serious.

Despite being sixty-four, I was remarkably healthy. I

never drank or smoked, and I tried to be relatively careful about diet and exercise. Honestly, the thought that it could be something as serious as Covid-19 never occurred to me; all I knew was I felt lousy and could hardly wait to get home.

I headed home to St. Louis on December 22, 2020. I think my suitcase had been loaded with bricks, it felt so freakishly heavy. It must have been noticeable to other passengers as they rushed to help me load and unload it from the overhead storage compartment. I could barely carry it as I changed flights for the final leg of my trip home. I tried not to cry, but I was past my endurance at that point. Huddled in my seat, double masked and miserable, the two-hour time change sadistically played mind games with me and added even more time to my flight.

After my husband, Don, picked me up from the airport and took over carrying my suitcase, we stopped at a neighborhood drugstore for cough drops before we got home. They didn't do much, but they helped a little bit.

The weight on my chest and the coughing was even more severe by that evening, so I decided to go to the urgent care facility near my house the next morning. Walking in to register, I was told I would be patient number thirty-three that day.

Number thirty-three!

I was advised to go home, and they would let me know when my appointment was coming up so I didn't have to waste time waiting at the clinic.

I dragged around the house waiting for the call, but no call came. Several hours later I took a nap, feeling feverish and unsettled. I woke up and realized it was 4:30 p.m. and I still hadn't received a call from urgent care. So, I called them.

Upon reaching the clinic, I was now patient number fourteen!

"So much for urgent care!" I complained. "I'm really sick!"

The voice on the other end of the phone hesitated, then said they would fit me in if I could get there in the next few minutes. I raced to get there.

As I walked through the clinic doors and identified myself, I was quickly ushered back to an exam room. A nurse took my vitals and kindly listened while I described my symptoms. She then administered tests for influenza and Covid-19. As I awaited my test results, I lay on the exam table exhausted. I have no idea how long I waited, as I lost all sense of time. I think I fell asleep. Then the nurse returned with the test results.

"Well, you don't have the flu …"

I waited for her to continue, but she stopped speaking.

"I have Covid?" I choked out, shocked.

She nodded with a concerned look on her face.

Tears welled up as I tried to figure out what this might mean for my family and me. I didn't know where to start or what steps to take. How do you deal with something like this?

Although Covid-19 was virulent in the United States, vaccines hadn't been made available yet. Everyone was taking precautions by following mask mandates and trying to stay safe. But most of the people I knew with Covid-19 had only experienced flulike symptoms. But I certainly didn't feel like this was the flu.

I was given an IV with antibiotics, after which I drove myself home. Don was not happy with me since I'd taken so long at the clinic without notifying him; frankly, I never even thought about it. By that time, I was lost in my concerns about what to do next and puzzled as to how to deal with it all. Since I had no idea what to expect, I laid around at home, hoping the solution would come to me. It didn't.

While I had been out of town, my dear hubby Don had decorated the Christmas tree and put up some decorations to welcome me home. It looked very pretty, I appreciated the gesture, but I just wasn't in the Christmas spirit. I painstakingly brought the Christmas village that would sit on the shelves in our kitchen up from the basement.

Those steps just about did me in. I found I didn't care about the village, didn't want to unbox it, didn't want to decide where to place the houses this year. The lethargy and fever left me not feeling like myself at all; it overwhelmed me.

Telling Kari, I knew she blamed herself for bringing me out to visit her, assuming I'd caught it out in LA. It was awful to hear her cry as she claimed it was all her fault. Thinking about it, I realized that I had most likely been exposed on my flight out to see her. It had been a full flight, and the young man next to me was all jittery and jolted himself awake every time he dozed off, which was often. At the time I'd assumed he was afraid of flying. Afterward, I realized he'd been very sick as he bolted off the plane almost as soon as it landed on the runway.

I shared that with Kari, trying to assure her that it was not her fault and I wasn't blaming her, but she wasn't convinced. Plus, I think she was upset that I had contracted Covid-19 despite their warnings and my precautions.

2

CHRISTMAS NIGHTMARE

Due to my diagnosis, my mom and my son, Ryan, and his wife, Megan, were uninvited from any celebrations, so Don and I spent Christmas Eve and Christmas Day alone. I forced myself to try to celebrate for Don's sake; I could tell he was excited to give me my presents.

Ever thoughtful, he gave me a huge vat of pretzels while I gave him a lawn sprinkler (not easy to wrap, by the way). After forty-two years of marriage, we still give romantic gifts …

Then he gave me a beautiful silver cuff bracelet that I just loved. Unfortunately, by that time I felt even worse than I had before. We took pictures of each other with our gifts. Looking at those photos now, I don't even recognize myself. Covid-19 had hit me hard and fast.

Christmas Day was a haze; truthfully, I spent most of it lying down, eating more cough drops to ease my sore throat, and trying to figure out how my prescribed steroid inhaler worked. It didn't.

I didn't realize at the time, but my lungs were quickly losing oxygen that was not being replaced and were filling up with fluid.

My cough worsened. Don tried to quarantine himself in the basement, but he also needed to stay with me to care

7

for me. He opted to stay with me, which is why he also got Covid-19.

Sometime in the late evening/early-morning hours on the twenty-sixth, I was so feverish I peeled off my sweat-soaked pajamas, wrapped myself in a blanket, and stood outside on our deck to cool off.

Don told me he heard a loud thump coming from the kitchen and came rushing in to find me in a heap on the floor. I couldn't, or didn't want to, get up. He called the hospital to see what he should do and was told to either contact our primary care physician or bring me into the emergency room. He chose the latter, having me pull on some hospital scrubs I often used as pajamas, and grabbed my coat and purse, and we were off.

Thankfully, the nearest hospital is less than a mile from my house. It was an odd experience to be rushing to the ER in the middle of the night/early morning when everyone else in town was asleep. The Christmas lights everywhere were especially surreal; how could my neighbors celebrate when I was so sick?

Don dropped me off at the emergency room entrance while he parked the car, assuming he could sit in the waiting room, and then he would just bring me home afterward.

According to Don, that was the last time he saw me; hospital protocol didn't allow anyone to be with a Covid-19 patient, so he had to experience all this alone. And so did I.

Ultimately, we wouldn't see each other again for almost three months.

3

ICU

As soon as I walked in, I was met by a friendly nurse who, upon seeing my scrubs/pajamas, asked me where I worked. I sheepishly explained that I was wearing my pajamas. I was taken to an exam room past the double doors and instructed to lie on the gurney while several IVs were administered. While waiting I decided to notify some friends.

Text to Stephanie

You're going to love this. I'm at the hospital in the ICU. I went early this morning 'cuz I felt like I was suffocating. I'm not calling 'cuz talking too much makes me cough. So that's all I know for now. Don't worry. I'm staying for a few days. No, Don can't be here. I'm not up to chatting right now. Why don't I check in later?

Terrible night last night with so many beeping machines. I'm on 90 percent administered oxygen and they want me under my own steam. Can't talk much 'cuz I have to save my breath. I can't believe this.

Text to April

Guess who has Covid-19? Meeeeeeeee. I feel like craaaaap. I was hoping it was strep or the flu. I'm really tired. I'm going to look over a few more posts and then collapse. Love you but I'm not hugging or kissing you.

Text from April

I can't believe you made your flight back. They usually burn people at the stake on airlines.

Text to Bonnie

I just wanted to let you know I'm in the hospital with Covid-19. Got here early this morning and they put me in the ICU. The nurse is keeping Don updated so if you want 70 percent accurate information you can call him.

Text to Mary

I'm at the hospital in the ICU since early this morning. They said if I'd waited any longer, I'd have needed a ventilator. I'm on oxygen and they're taking really good care of me. I feel so much better already. But I've never been given so many drugs in my life! No phone calls 'cuz I have to save my breath.

Text to Kari

I'm really tired. I think the only thing they haven't done for me is paint my toenails.

Text to Ryan

I was given 3 IVs to help. One was just fluids to help with dehydration, one was a steroid, and one was for pain.

Text to Mary K

Guess who's in the hospital with Covid-19? Yes, that's right, ME! I think I caught it on an overbooked flight to see Kari. Barely made it to the hospital yesterday a.m. But all my vitals are great except for oxygen level.

Text to Michele

Went to the hospital yesterday with Covid-19. Almost didn't make it, my oxygen levels were dangerously low. I'm not supposed to talk. Don would love it.

Don notified Kari and Ryan.

Text from Ryan

Dad called me and was so weird. We'd had a workday scheduled. When he called, he said he couldn't come to the studio and help me; he'd been exposed to someone with Covid-19, someone I knew: my mother.

Text from Don

I was trying to break it to him gently.

Ryan

It definitely was a bummer. I remember thinking, "We were right about that, but I don't want to be right about that." I was upset, disappointed, and frustrated because I hadn't wanted Mom to go in the first place.

The problem with Covid-19 is that we are all at the mercy of other people. Anytime you go out in public, you can only hope other people are being careful. And if they aren't, there's nothing you can do about it.

For all the energy you put into your own safety and the safety of others, it just takes one person, like the guy on the plane. He passed it to Mom, and he gets to go home.

Everyone gathered by the phone, and together they placed a conference call to the hospital for an update. They were told I was very, very sick and thankful Don brought me in since without immediate treatment I wouldn't have lasted much longer.

Apparently, during this time the oxygen tubes in my nose were making me claustrophobic, so I would try to push them away in my sleep. The doctors administered Remdesivir immediately along with sedatives and fluids to keep me hydrated, but it was not effective for me. It was scary.

December 27

Due to the heavy doses of medications, I don't remember much of my early hospitalization. It seemed as if there were people everywhere, constantly milling around, taking my vitals, and drawing blood. The seriousness of my condition never really occurred to me as I joked with the medical staff. I just assumed they would fix me up and send me home. So did Don as he told the kids, "I'm not worried, so you shouldn't be worried."

Gareth

When Don told us Karen had Covid-19, we were alarmed, obviously. But since she was healthy and had no comorbidities, we figured she would be able to take care of herself and get through it safely. By this time, Kari and I had also contracted Covid-19, probably from Karen, so we were miserable. Our Covid-19 test results were mixed; I tested positive, while Kari's results were negative even though she was as sick as I was.

In the meantime, Don had to self-quarantine since he'd been exposed to me at home. He notified his place of employment, then set about texting friends and family. It was too difficult for him to be sure he'd contacted everyone, plus he had also contracted Covid-19 and felt terrible. For that reason, he would post everything he knew from that day on social media. Friends and family eagerly waited for daily updates.

One close family friend, Stephanie, contacted people I knew on social media, while many people shared our situation and asked *their* friends and family members to pray for us. She and her wife raced to the pharmacy to get meds for Don and delivered them to our house and helped in so many ways.

Michele, another friend, worked diligently to have her circle of prayer warriors put me first on their lists; she also watched over Don while he had Covid-19, going out of her way to provide him with effective vitamins to help him recover.

Mary gave Don a card and some helpful gifts during this time. Many people made sure Don took care of himself, dropping off meals and calling and texting often to check in.

Don on Social Media
My wife Karen is in the hospital with Covid-19. It

is not being kind to her. I would ask that you pray for her and the folks that take care of her. She is stable, but her breathing is hampered by the infection. With oxygen she is at 90 percent capacity. Doctors feel she is reacting positively to treatment. However, the progress is slow. I have been exposed and am in quarantine. My test results will not be in for several days. Thank you for your prayers and warm wishes.

After testing positive for Covid-19, Don became progressively sicker throughout the week.

December 28

Don on Social Media

The doctors today say that her oxygen levels are not holding the way they want them to. They changed her tube to a mask with the hopes that it will increase her oxygen supply. That's what I know at this time. Thanks again for your prayers.

December 29

Don on Social Media

An update on my wife. As of 3:30 this afternoon, Karen had a coughing spell that dropped her oxygen level down to 70. The doctors were not pleased with how slowly she was regaining her oxygen level, so they put her on a ventilator and inserted a feeding tube.

I dreamed that there was a tightly zippered suitcase sitting in the middle of an empty courtyard. I had been looking at it for quite some time. At long last, someone came to unzip it, after which I thought, "Oh good, now I can breathe."

Kari

I got a call from my dad on the twenty-ninth and he's crying, very upset, and he said, "They just put your mother on a ventilator." So, she was now on a ventilator with a feeding tube and was fully sedated.

Gareth and I realized this was much worse than we were being told; it was much more severe, so we needed to get involved. I contacted an old friend of ours, Dr. Rammy Yogendra, who we have known since we all lived in New York years ago.

Rammy was an anesthesiologist at a hospital for a while, then he moved into private practice and entrepreneurship.

But when Covid-19 hit, he began working extensively with severe Covid-19 patients in clinical settings. He was also tuned into cutting-edge research. There's a lot we don't understand about the virus, the emerging therapies and treatments, the different forms it takes, and the syndromes that characterize severe Covid-19. We knew we needed his help, and he willingly gave it.

We had a few long phone conversations with him. Rammy then sent us an email with resources for Mom and what should take priority. He also impressed upon us the reality that this was going to be a very unpleasant experience for everyone, and that we would have to put our gloves on and fight to the very end. (VERY END?)

After our initial phone call, Rammy responded with an email:

Your mom is most likely in the "cytokine storm." It is a hyperimmune condition, that is the reason her lungs are filled with fluid right now. The goal of treatment is using "immunomodulating" medications to redirect the hyperinflammation away from the organs and "calm the storm down." Cytokines are messenger proteins secreted by immune cells to coordinate responses and for an unknown reason in some patients those signals go "nuts."

Drug A is pointless at this point. The hospital and doctors may consider steroids—but these can be more harmful than good for some patients. What you DO NOT want is the hospital keeping her on a ventilator and hoping she recovers on her own. Some patients do recover on their own, but my approach is why not give them something else to aid in that recovery?

Text from Kari

I'm sure you're resting, just letting you know how much I love you.

I know you can't see this, but I love you so much. Please stay with us, I can't live without my mom.

You're my best friend.

And I'm sorry.

Kari

Rammy also told us we had to do everything in

our power to not just help the doctors but also push them and motivate them to think outside the standard of care for Covid-19, because that standard is, frankly, to stabilize patients, give them supportive care, but let the virus run its course naturally. Then let the patients get better on their own; if they don't, then they usually don't make it.

Gareth

It's important to mention that there was a general monoclonal antibody available to the US at the time. However, access to it was extremely limited because it was an infusion, was relatively unknown, and they had no designated place in the hospital where they could administer it.

Monoclonal antibodies attack the spike proteins of the Covid-19 virus, specifically designed to target the CCR5 receptor. The CCR5 receptor is one way Covid-19 hijacks the immune system, causing this hyperinflammatory syndrome, a runaway inflammation, especially around the lungs. This causes the lungs to be damaged and underdeveloped.

However, the monoclonal antibody purchased and distributed by the government was intended to be administered within seven days of initial Covid-19 diagnosis, early in the virus.

We spoke to some doctors in several emergency rooms, and they didn't know the difference in the monoclonal antibodies we were talking about, so they were just giving us a swift hard NO because it had been past seven days. That was a huge struggle for us, trying to explain that there was another monoclonal antibody, Drug B, available.

Don on Social Media

We have been in contact with a doctor who Kari and Gareth know who deals directly with Covid-19 patients. He has recommended some stuff to talk to the hospital about, and see if they would change treatment since the drugs they are giving her now are not doing what they're supposed to do. If they were, she wouldn't have needed a ventilator. Karen has a long battle ahead of her that's not going to be easy for any of us. All we can do is hope and pray.

Kari

After we received Dr. Rammy's emails, we talked via phone. He said, "Let's get a game plan together," so we decided to talk in the morning, and call the doctors and get going. Gareth and I reached out to her doctor at the hospital, Dr. Q, who was a pulmonologist on duty the morning Mom was admitted to the ICU. Dr. Q was her main attending, making most of the clinical decisions about Mom's care. We spoke with several night shift personnel as well.

By the way, we were doing this remotely, since Gareth and I live in California. We communicated by phone, video, and conference calls, which made everything so much more difficult. Dad was Mom's primary proxy and was involved in all but the most intense conversations.

Gareth

Initially, the need for information and decision making was very extensive; however, since Don was also Covid-19 positive, it became harder to involve him as time went on.

4

NEXT MOVE

Kari

Rammy told us we needed to track her progress daily and ask these questions:

1. Blood gas. What is PO_2, PCO_2, and bicarbonate? What is her pH?

2. Chest x-rays, what does it show? (She received chest x-rays every single day she was in each hospital. Once the fluid began to clear out, the x-rays were reduced to every few days. We weren't given the results daily, as not everyone at the hospital was trained to read x-rays.)

3. Ventilator settings: what is the FiO_2? And how much is the PEEP? These were the two indicators we were trending. FiO_2 (fractional inspired oxygen) is the amount of oxygen they are supplying to her lungs so that she can keep oxygenating. When we breathe air, the FiO_2 is 21 percent.

Mom was being given FiO_2 of 80, which would sometimes fluctuate down to 60. We would get hopeful when the number would drop, but then it would jump back up. When she began to hold steady at FiO_2

of 40 percent, we got so excited; after a while she didn't really need higher levels of FiO$_2$. Along with the FiO$_2$, we also monitored her PEEP, which stands for positive-end expiratory pressure. Typically, when a patient is on a ventilator, PEEP is applied to prevent tiny air sacs, called alveoli, from collapsing. Since Mom's alveoli were filled with fluid from inflammation, upward of a PEEP of fifteen was initially applied. As she improved, we observed the doctors decreasing the amount of PEEP she required to maintain adequate oxygenation and ventilation. This was a positive and exciting sign that the insult to her lungs was slowly resolving.

4. Is she being prone? Prone is a positioning of the patient on their stomach; they recently learned that Covid-19 patients respond well to proning.
5. Are they alternating being prone with the supine and side-to-side positioning?

Supine positioning is returning the patient to lying on their back, with the addition to the side-to-side movement. The theory is that alternating these positions uses gravity to move the fluid around in the lungs, thus preventing the fluids from collecting in one area. Otherwise, the gathering fluids would create infected areas that wouldn't heal. It also allows some air into certain parts of the lungs to avoid suppression.

This positioning wasn't done the first few days; she was on a ventilator for twenty-four to forty-eight hours before they started proning her, at our insistence. The nurses reported that Mom really liked the prone position, so they kept her prone for sixteen hours a day.

6. Liver function enzymes (LFT) and kidney function enzymes (BUN) and creatinine."

On December 30, we made our first telephone contact with Dr. Q. Dad was also on the call, and Gareth and I jumped right in asking if Mom was prone and what was going on. We started to dive into Drug B talks. Rammy was often quietly guiding us by text on what questions to ask and what answers to accept.

Right away we knew that it was moment-to-moment, and we had to move quickly. Dr. Q agreed. It was a critical time, as Mom had just been ventilated and she was having a hard time. Now was the time to explore any and all options, thinking ahead in case the current treatments didn't work. Our next option was Drug B, which required special permission from the FDA to administer.

Dr. Q was not familiar with Drug B. Might this medication work? We gave Dr. Q an overview and followed up with a very concise email, focused on highlighted information because the hospitals were just running ragged. We couldn't just assume the doctor had time to leave his other patients to read these documents. Therefore, we condensed them as tightly as we could so that he didn't have to do research he didn't have time for.

Rammy had access to doctors and researchers connected to Covid-19 studies and clinical trials, which was a real benefit in this crisis. These resources were crucial to Mom's care, guiding us in what action to take. This information was invaluable; there was nothing else we could do from so far away.

Gareth

Additionally, as Don also had Covid-19, Rammy provided his medical expertise to aid in his recovery.

Dr. Q's general stance was that experimental or investigative treatments really didn't have a place in the hospital system within which he worked. Apparently, there's a standard of care in the current healthcare system; early in the pandemic there was a vaccine, but it wasn't as effective as promised. As a result, they removed it from their protocol and have been medically conservative ever since. So, he was rather stubborn against the possibility of getting the drugs until we explained our connections that would make it feasible. Reluctantly, Dr. Q told us he didn't love the idea, but he wouldn't stand in our way. He also informed us that part of the reason the hospital is so hesitant is they don't have a review board to consult in instances like this.

Kari

In order to receive permission to use an experimental medication, the attending hospital must have their investigative review board (IRB) look over your request to see if it's a reasonable treatment. If they say it's okay, you can use it; if not, you're out of luck. They say it's due to liability concerns.

Dr. Q told us that the hospital where Mom was didn't have a review board. We asked him, "How then do you get the medications you need to treat patients?" to which he replied, "We don't." Because this wasn't a teaching hospital, it didn't have an IRB. In the past, Dr. Q had tried to obtain RLF-100 and was unable to do so, whether due to administrative or bureaucratic hurdles or perhaps the patient didn't qualify for it. Therefore, he must have chosen to follow the hospital protocols and do what he already knew to do.

Gareth began reaching out to people at the much larger healthcare facility in St. Louis that, thankfully, has its own protocol for care.

Gareth

So, I randomly called their office and administrative board and spoke to someone there. The woman on the phone was very helpful, especially since this was such a time-sensitive situation.

She directed us to a commercial IRB that hires itself out to people who are doing studies or individuals in situations like ours.

Megan also jumped in to assist Kari and Gareth in any way she could. She would research the different ways to help them, finding phone numbers and constantly sharing what she had found.

Kari

At this point we had the IRB figured out, we had Rammy helping us, Dr. Q was treating Mom at the hospital, we were trying to make Drug B available should Mom need it, and now the doctor wouldn't cooperate.

Rammy ultimately emailed the CEO of the company that has Drug B. Rammy wrote him, as well as several other doctors who were researching this:

I am writing regarding my close friend, Kari Wasoba, whose mother is currently intubated and on a ventilator in an ICU in Missouri. I spoke to Kari and her family extensively about the potential of Drug B, and they have decided to pursue it through the FDA eIND.

The ICU doctor is skeptical and hesitant but is willing to pursue this. However, the roadblock we have encountered is the hospital does not have an IRB. I didn't know if this is a situation your company has encountered with other patients and if you had any advice on how to proceed. I think we might be able to get everyone on board if we get this IRB hurdle out of the way.

Thanks,
Ram Yogendra MD, MPH

The next day Gareth wrote:

Thank you, Ram, for putting us in touch. On the IRB front, we can engage a commercial IRB to facilitate this:

https://www.wcgir.com/services/expanded-access-compassionate-use/.

This option was recommended to me by IRB's associate director, and I've also talked to WCGIRB client services.

Based on your past experiences getting this drug to Covid-19 patients, what steps can I take to a) reduce the doctor's paperwork/time required so this is not an undue burden on him, and b) ensure that it is efficient? Thank you all!

Kari

It was after nine o'clock at night when we decided to call the hospital to speak to Mom's evening ICU physician.

We said, "We're still working on getting Drug B, but we wanted to talk to you about giving Mom a medication called Drug C." We explained that it was FDA approved for scabies, for parasites; the only side effects Drug C had were nausea and diarrhea. And we really didn't care if she soiled herself if it meant she was going to get better. It had a lot going for it in terms of safety. It was also used worldwide in many developing countries, especially as an antiparasitic. Once Covid-19 started, it was a drug of convenience because it was readily available and affordable.

When a "cytokine storm" is active in the lungs, the white blood cells travel there to combat it. However, those white blood cells start fighting each other in confusion. Because of that, the actual Covid-19 and pneumonia are not being targeted.

When a patient is given Drug C designed for human usage, not veterinary Drug C, many of the cells fighting in the lungs learn that parasites are active in the body. This information causes them to leave the lungs to focus on the parasite. This clears some of the storm and gives the body a better chance at fighting the infection present with Covid-19.

So, that said, it didn't seem like it would do any harm, and would hopefully have a preventative as well as an anti-inflammatory effect. The ICU physician said she saw no harm in it, but since she wasn't Mom's primary physician, she would discuss it with Dr. Q in the morning. Our main goal here was just to buy Mom as much time as possible until more information was gathered as to what specific treatment she would need.

Don on social media:

Last night while praying, I was shaking so hard. All I could do was cry out to God, and the words "Hold me, Jesus" came to mind and became part of my prayer.

The power of your love and prayers have indeed held me and my family up. Karen is not out of the woods yet.

Kari

The overnight ICU physician and Dr. Q met and agreed to give her Drug C. Mom received her first intravenous dose around lunchtime on December 31.

Something to note about this medication is that it takes two doses to be effective; the second dose should be given anywhere from five to seven days after the first dose.

While we were happy Mom was getting Drug C, we didn't want to just rely on that, so we kept pursuing permission to use Drug B, an experimental drug that required special permission from the FDA. We didn't want to overlook anything.

Gareth then wrote Dr. Q, who had been cc'd on all our emails to the other doctors. We said, "Here we go, here's what we need, please send it. Thank you so much." We filled out any forms that might be required so it was ready to go if necessary.

This was at 9:05 p.m. on New Year's Eve. There was added stress and urgency, and now it was New Year's Eve. What if everybody shut off their phones over the holiday? That didn't happen; we were very grateful that these doctors stayed close to their phones and were helping us.

We felt like everyone had the same sense of urgency as we did to make this happen.

Don on social media:

This morning we got some good news. Her ventilator oxygen intake was reduced from 90 percent to 50 percent overnight. That is exciting stuff. On top of that, her doctors administered one of the drugs we had been advocating, Drug C. We are hoping that we can get her off the ventilator soon.

I am still shaking, but the arms of my Savior are still holding Karen and me and reminding all of us that our hope is in Him. Thank you for your continued prayers."

Kari

Our family had a video chat with Mom on New Year's Eve. We all met: Ryan and Megan, Gareth and me, Dad, and of course Mom. She couldn't talk to us, obviously, but we talked to her and each other. Megan had typed up the poison scene from *The Princess Bride* and we performed it; at midnight we did the countdown together, and Ryan played "Auld Lang Syne" on guitar.

Ryan

What was weird was that this was the first time since college that I didn't have a gig on New Year's Eve. I didn't have to run off; I could be with Mom and the rest of the family.

Kari

We never knew if Mom could hear us or not, but we wanted to have a visual and say, "Mommy, we love you."

Apparently, this video chat was the first time they had seen me on the ventilator. It was a shock to all of them, yet they continued signing on every evening to catch up, play music, or talk to me, all the while seeing me unresponsive and looking worse each day. No one could believe this was happening.

Occasionally, Don would invite a friend to join the chat; invariably, they all did. I consider that an extreme act of love from them all and I am grateful.

Several friends took screenshots of me on the video. They

were afraid this would be their last view of me. Seeing the photos later, I was in disbelief at how bad I looked. I looked dead. This was how they wanted to remember me?

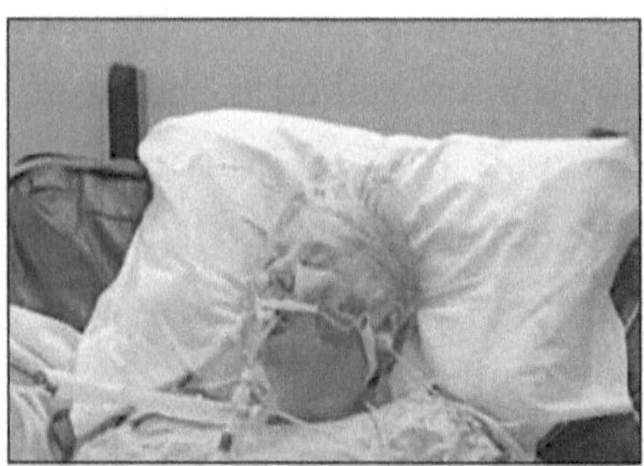

I had to be intubated twice

Kari

All through this Covid-19 experience, we spent an hour or more each day talking to Mom, talking at her, using an iPad for video calls. Over time, we realized that a nurse was having to hold the iPad in front of Mom while we had our chats. This led us to purchase an iPad stand to free up the nurses' time. Ultimately, the stand was donated to the ICU unit. We played a lot of John Denver and Harry Styles and included our own favorites. Ryan would play his guitar, and we would talk among ourselves. We wanted to keep her mind active and for her to know she wasn't alone, that we were with her through this.

Text from Michele
Keep fighting this, Karen.

I had the weirdest dream. In it, my son, Ryan, was in the military and doing well. In fact, he was enlisted to be an admiral in the army! (The army doesn't have admirals ...). It was New Year's Eve, and he had to fly a huge plane to the North Pole. I was on the flight, and I wanted to see "my son the admiral." I climbed up the narrow stairs to the cockpit and found that he and the head flight attendant had set up a tiki bar and were serving drinks! They had streamers and coconut decorations and even had Hawaiian music playing. The flight attendant had a cigarette hanging out of her mouth as she expertly poured drinks. I sat down at the bar, and Ryan said, "Mom, what are you doing here? You don't drink." I said, "I don't care, make me something." And much to my surprise, he did!

The plane landed and rolled up to a stark stone monument and hooked up to it. The sky was extremely dark and quiet, save for the humming from the plane's engine. For the next twenty-four hours, Ryan's assignment was to monitor the world and make sure it kept turning on its axis. The sky remained dark; it felt cold and desolate. Then the dream ended.

Kari

Ultimately, we are grateful we didn't have to go so far as to take legal action to use the medication, although we did consult with a family friend who is a lawyer. We wanted to know our options regarding a state statute called Right to Try, which gives hospital patients the right to have access to experimental or investigated drug therapies that are for compassionate use.

We also avoided legal action because we realized early on that getting a lawyer involved in any kind of legal action or a letter from some office would be a good way to shut down the communication we'd established with Mom's doctors.

Obviously, doctors will stop talking to you and not want to help you anymore if you threaten to sue them.

Incidentally, when we requested a new Covid-19 test, the doctor on duty told us that the local hospital is often very limited on how many Covid-19 tests they can use so they must ration them. But she approved it because she felt the result would really help Mom. The doctor said it wasn't something they could do all the time, which demonstrated how limited in supplies the hospitals were nine months into the pandemic.

Text from April

I prayed last night every time I got up. Thanks to my bladder, you were covered in a lot of prayers. You're welcome.

Did I tell you I hate this for you? No? I hate this for you, Don, and your kids. I know you are proud of your family. But they are amazing! They are faithful, prayerful, and fighting for you!

In another dream, I became aware of a bitter coldness. I found myself in a northern city that was desolate, almost deserted. It seemed as if it had been ravaged by war. I had a few things with me but not much with which to survive. I entered a dark, cement room where the few windows were without glass, so there was no warmth at all. Hunkering down with my arms wrapped around my body, my first thought was, "How am I going to survive this?" My second thought was, "*Of course* I'm going to survive this!" I was almost disappointed when the dream was over in that I couldn't prove my intent to thrive and survive.

Don's December 30 post

Covid-19 update on me and Karen. Karen's condition is stable but serious. Her body is in the "cytokine storm" phase, which is a hyperimmune condition that has caused her lungs to fill with fluid. Her last dose of Drug A will be tomorrow morning. We are in the process of negotiating an experimental treatment at this stage. Our hope is that we can get through the hospital protocols asap, but doing that is like an act of Congress. Please pray for health and wisdom. I am at the tail end of this. My symptoms have decreased, and I am almost feeling human again.

Text from April

It's 10:30 at night. God's timing is perfect. I keep thinking you need to be healed quickly. I am wondering if while you are sleeping you know/feel the prayers of your friends and the presence of God. The waiting for your health to turn the corner is gut-wrenching, yet I am strangely peaceful and thankful for more time to pray for you. Get well soon. I want more late-night memes from you.

Throughout this entire experience, I had weird dreams, each seeming to coincide with whatever was happening around me. Many of them also placed me in an extremely cold environment.

I dreamed I was in a hospital bed with many dark-haired women milling around me, laughing and talking. The room was half dark and half light, but there were no windows. When it was day, my bed would be rotated toward the light, and then toward the dark in the evening. The women were hired to tend to me, but they interacted more with each other than with me. It seemed as if I was a good excuse for them to have fun together, and more and more women came into the room, laughing and joking. I was unable to move or interact with them, and I wondered if they were ignoring me on purpose.

These women were getting dressed for church on Sunday morning and intended to leave me there. I remember one woman leaned over me to check something and then most of them left.

This seemed to go on for several days, me just lying there and these women coming and going. I was frustrated and aggravated; I didn't know if it was really day or night, and I had no idea where I was.

I finally came to believe that instead of being in a hospital, I was in a shabby hotel room with the windows blocked out so I couldn't see. From the hospital bed, I accused them of trying to cheat my family by having a great time at my family's expense, scamming them by treating me in a fake hospital.

I know now that I was in fact in a *real* hospital, and nurses came in to check on me regularly. They would converse with me, although I was unresponsive, which made me imagine that everyone was having a fun time but me!

Kari

The researchers had all encouraged us to have Dr. Q resubmit paperwork for permission to use experimental medicines if it came to that, and we would see what happened.

New Year's Day, January 1, 2021, we called Dr. Q, aware that he'd been following along on the email chain with the other doctors, knowing that Mom qualified for Drug B. His attitude had completely changed. He now refused to redo and resubmit the paperwork.

We were angry. We had to confront him, asking him why he wouldn't do it. He said he wasn't going to lie on the paperwork. But we weren't asking him to lie; we were asking him to update the information. Just submit it and let the FDA decide.

Yes, we said, but you were on the email chain. They said it would be okay; it just had to prove that she still actively had Covid-19.

Dr. Q disagreed, stating that was not the intention of the paperwork.

Apparently, his belief was if he signed and submitted the form, he would be misrepresenting himself, even though the form had no factual inaccuracies.

We argued with him, really got into it. We said Mom's stats were bad enough, we need to do something. During our discussion, he reminded us we were only doing this as a coping mechanism. That instead of fighting for Mom, we should just stay at home and sit in our feelings, although we had never been emotional on any of these calls. Yes, we'd been talking to him a lot, speaking with a sense of urgency. Yes, it's important, but the accusation that this was a coping mechanism was unbelievable. In essence, he was telling us to give up and let her die.

Prior to this meeting, Gareth and I had been talking about having Mom moved to the bigger hospital in St. Louis, mostly for the IRB. No matter what, we wanted Mom out of her current hospital.

While still in talks with Dr. Q, we mentioned Drug C and how Mom showed no improvement after getting the first dose, so she probably needed the second one, which was due the next day.

I said, "If you won't do the paperwork, can you at least promise that she'll get her second dose of Drug C tomorrow?"

Dr. Q hinted that he wouldn't do that either. That's when he told us we should expect that Drug C was killing her.

He was saying that what we'd convinced them to do was making her worse.

So now he wouldn't do the paperwork for Drug B, and he wouldn't give Mom her second dose of Drug C.

After a very intense conversation, during which we kept remarkably calm, considering this doctor just told us we were basically killing our mom and we needed to prepare ourselves because we would have to live with it, Dr. Q's tone changed. He said, "I'm not saying I won't give it to her. I'm just saying that you're not considering that what you're doing is what's hurting her."

Dr. Q assured us that many families reacted as we were, desperately seeking help for their ailing loved ones. He suggested we go home and deal with our feelings over Mom's impending death.

To which we replied, "Please just give her the Drug C tomorrow."

5

ANOTHER MOVE,
ANOTHER HOSPITAL

Kari

Lesson learned: aggressive treatment may not be the best course of action, but mere supportive care wasn't exactly helping. Dr. Q agreed to give Mom the second dose of Drug C the next day, but no, he would not fill out the paperwork to the FDA for potential use of Drug B.

Thankfully, by the end of this communication, Dr. Q decided to be open about the possibility of using Drug B if necessary. Once he understood that the researcher working on Drug B was willing to change the protocol language, widening the requirements to include more qualified patients, he was much more comfortable.

It was amazing that the researcher who helped create the written protocol for FDA approval for Drug B was potentially going to change the requirement for use of the drug for Covid-19 to make it more readily available for emergency use. Thus, possibly saving more lives.

In a new dream, I was in a small rural town, in an old church building. I had decided we were going to revive an old tradition of baking apple tarts every Sunday morning for the townspeople. Soon, I noticed that my helpers were disappearing, one by one.

I discovered they were being murdered, wrapped in plastic, and shoved down a chute to the basement. None of the other helpers mentioned the missing people. I tried to get help, but no one would listen to me.

Seeing Kari on a video chat, I told her about it and asked her to send help. She wouldn't act on it. I told her several times, but she ignored my pleas.

I got so angry, I said, "As God is my witness, I will never talk to you again!"

Kari didn't react, didn't cry. She responded, "I'm sorry you feel that way."

I questioned her about it later because I felt terrible about acting like that. She assured me that it had never happened; therefore, it must have been part of my dream. I hope.

December 27, 2020

Don

Update Karen Wasoba

Late last night, after our discussion with Karen's doctor, it was decided that as a precautionary measure, Karen would be moved to a larger hospital in St. Louis.

Her condition, though stable, has not changed. The fear is, if she goes backward, the ICU unit she's in now would not have the resources to help her. The downtown facility has far more resources and is able to respond if her condition were to worsen. Right now, Karen is holding steady. She made the trip to the hospital without incident. There has been no change to her condition overnight. My little lady has a way to go.

We continue to see God's Hand in her care. Please continue to pray for her and her doctors and all my family as well. Your support is felt and greatly appreciated.

Gareth

That night, Don received a phone call from Dr. Q, saying Karen was going to be moved as soon as there was a bed available in the cardiothoracic ICU.

The scene then changed; I was in the same bed in the same room, but it was now housed in an ambulance whose engine never shut off (probably the ambulance ride to the other hospital). I was to be part of a pioneering project that used the engine sound and slight movement of the machine to soothe patients.

At first, it made sense, but soon I realized that it certainly didn't soothe *me!* It seemed endless and pointless. When it ended, it was just done, which underscored how useless this experiment had been in the first place. No one was interested in the results of the experiment; in fact, a nurse walked around the hospital grounds with me in tow, looking for an administrator to report the findings. Still dreaming, I finally told her I was done with this and walked away.

Kari

The newer hospital had a lot more space, a lot

more equipment, some advanced departments the smaller hospital didn't have. When asked why the move, we were told since Mom wasn't improving, she might need ECMO, which was available there.

ECMO is extracorporeal membrane oxygenation, in which they remove the patient's blood into a machine that reoxygenates it and returns it to the patient. It's an invasive procedure; the survival rate for ECMO patients is around 30 percent. At 9:58 p.m., January 2, Mom was transferred to their cardiothoracic ICU.

Gareth

Kari and I, by this point, were also feeling kind of under the weather, starting to lose our sense of smell. We were tested that day, and I ended up testing positive and Kari tested negative although she felt as sick as I did. Kari never did test positive for Covid-19; later we learned that the company that had tested us had about 20 percent false negative samples.

Though she tested negative, we both needed the same care.

January 1, 2021

Kari

Thankfully, Mom didn't need the ECMO after all.

Dr. S was Mom's new attending physician, so we set about researching him and his qualifications. Apparently, he was very much involved in Covid-19 clinical research, so he knew the difference between the various monoclonal antibodies. We knew we'd have to start the Drug B process from scratch, but we also knew that this bigger hospital had more access to experimental or investigative treatments.

It was still difficult for us because Mom was being moved because she wasn't doing well. However, once at the bigger hospital the quality of care improved.

We contacted Dr. S right away and came away knowing Mom was in knowledgeable hands. We had a good feeling about Dr. S. We brought up Drugs B and C, saying Mom was supposed to receive her second dose of Drug C before she was moved but she hadn't.

The former doctor, Dr. Q, had never called in the order.

We told Dr. S we wanted this, we really believed in this, plus she'd already been given the first dose. He was reasonable, saying, "That's not usually our standard of care, but you're right, I see no danger in giving her Drug C. I will make sure she gets it."

Her second dose was given on Monday, January 3. What a huge relief!

Next, we mentioned Drug B. We told Dr. S we had been pursuing the medication prior to moving to his hospital, and we already had a letter of approval to apply for its use, and we asked if he would be willing to resubmit the paperwork as her current doctor.

Dr. S. didn't shut us down but was clear he wasn't very comfortable about it.

He wasn't familiar with the research on Drug B, although he was aware that it existed. Gareth went into detail regarding its properties and usage, after which the doctor requested our research materials. Basically, Dr. S told us he wasn't ruling it out, but he wasn't going to act on it immediately.

"Please, please, give me time to do what I do, and for us to do what we do here. If she doesn't improve or things get bad, we can look into this. But give me a minute to do my thing first," he replied.

We felt good about that conversation, like he had listened to us. We immediately wrote him about and forwarded him the information we mentioned earlier.

Dr. S. responds

Dear Gareth and Kari,

The data you sent me is very preliminary. This would not be a drug I would come close to committing my patients to.

In the interim, I have also reached out to an emergency medicine specialist in the study of viral respiratory diseases, including influenza and Covid-19, to see what he has to say about this drug.

I hope this is helpful.

Dr. S.

During all of this, my dad was also fighting Covid-19. He was pale, almost white. His cough was getting worse, he was not feeling well, and his oxygen levels were not great. We were tracking his oxygen levels with a pulse oximeter at home, and it didn't look good.

Always the dad, he promised he would go to

urgent care first thing in the morning. We didn't want him to wait; we now understood that every hour matters when dealing with Covid-19. Gareth called him and did some cajoling, urged him to go to the emergency room immediately. He wanted Dad to think urgently about his health, especially since someone he cares about was sick. Dad wasn't thinking about himself. He's someone who could be sick and continue going about his daily life, hoping to get better on his own. He's a tough guy.

Dad is very old school and genuinely tough. However, two years before this, he had pneumonia around the holidays, and we forced him to go to urgent care. It was very severe at that time. So, we were understandably concerned about him.

Eventually Dad agreed to go to the hospital, more to calm us down than anything else. He was diagnosed with Covid-19 pneumonia. Doctors gave him oxygen, took x-rays, and gave him Toradol for pain. Then he was sent home.

We sent the x-rays to Rammy to make sure everything was fine because I couldn't handle another parent in the hospital with Covid-19. Rammy confirmed Covid-19 pneumonia. Even though the local ER doctors told Dad he would be fine, Rammy sent the x-rays to his own dad, also a long-standing clinical doctor, for a second opinion. His dad confirmed Rammy's diagnosis and that it needed immediate treatment.

By January 4, my dad's cough became even worse,

and he had pneumonia in his lungs. We sat down with Dad for a telehealth appointment.

The telehealth doctor prescribed Drug C immediately (since it wasn't a hospital setting) and Symbicort, which is a corticosteroid in inhaler form.

The next day, January 5, Dad notified his primary care physician of his Covid-19 diagnosis. The PCP also prescribed a Z-Pak and half a sleeping pill to be taken every other day since Dad wasn't sleeping due to all the stress.

On top of everything else, we were tracking Dad; we were psychotically checking in with him about every two hours. We wanted to know how he was feeling, did he take his meds, what was his oxygen level? We were the pulse oximeter police.

Soon, Dad improved and recovered fully. But remember, Gareth and I also had contracted Covid-19, we had the standard symptoms of fever and loss of taste and smell. I had a rapid heartbeat and shortness of breath.

But we didn't pursue any type of medication since we were so anxious and pumped with adrenaline dealing with everything. It was hard to tell if these were Covid-19 symptoms or a panic attack. And we slowly recovered.

January 5

Don on social media

Karen's temperature has dropped down a little bit. So, she's running a low-grade fever now instead of a 102-degree fever. They were able to lower her oxygen level intake to 40 percent. It appears that all her vital signs are holding solid. She is still not out of the woods, but she is holding firm. And that's a good thing.

This is a much larger facility, and it's harder to reach a doctor or nurse than the other hospital. It's difficult to reach anyone before noon. I might only be able to give one update a day, but I will keep you informed as best I can. Thank you all for your prayers! My breathing is easier. I feel like I'm getting more oxygen. Thanks again.

Update from Don

Karen has gone up and down a little bit during these past twenty-four hours, which is to be expected. At this point, all her vital signs are steady and holding firm. Her oxygen level is about 60, being taken in by the ventilator, and about 96 percent oxygen level in her lungs. She has viral pneumonia present, which they are dealing with as well. We are talking about our next stage of care for her, and the direction will be chosen within the next twenty-four hours.

A lot of you have asked about our kids. Kari and Gareth have a moderate case. We are thankful for the doctors who sent Karen to the larger hospital. It was a worrisome move at the time, but we see now it was the best thing they could do for her. Please continue to pray for Karen and my family. God bless you, and I'll let you know if anything new comes up.

January 5

Email from Dr. S

I have some updates.

1. *I contacted the Covid-19 specialist who says that the results (for Drug B) were too preliminary to try here. Given that the drug has no FDA EUA there would be no way to use it at our institution.*

2. *I have asked about three other trials here—given her duration of mechanical ventilation and recent positive result for secondary pneumonia, she would not be eligible for any trials.*

3. *Given the secondary pneumonia, I think treating her with immunomodulatory drugs is not advisable.*

4. *Importantly, she has made some incremental improvement. Her oxygen requirements have come down and we are not having to prone her today. Although we are not out of the woods yet and there is still a long way to go, we are definitely in a better place today than yesterday and the day before.*

Best wishes, S.

Kari

This was the first assessment of Mom's condition that wasn't poorly placed optimism. Dr. S. was citing improvement over the last few days since arriving at the St. Louis hospital. There was more access to better-trained staff with better equipment and newer facilities. She was now in the cardiothoracic ICU.

The medical staff administered many tests to find out which specific areas they needed to target with appropriate treatment. Apparently, there were more medical issues, besides the infection, that my body was experiencing.

I've included the complete list in Chapter 8.

Kari

Mom received her second dose of Drug C there. The doctor was right; she did have secondary pneumonia. In retrospect, that was probably the most dangerous phase of her illness. Because her lungs were trying to recover, she had some pulmonary fibrosis, which occurs when lung tissue becomes damaged and scarred. This scarred tissue makes breathing more difficult for the lungs to work properly.

This week her lung x-rays showed that there was some damage as well as a lot of fluid in her lungs. However, when a secondary infection is present, that's not the time to start modulating the immune system. It needs to be left to do its job.

At this point we felt more positive about her standard of care and didn't push back on their decision making. It was better Mom improve this way than just give her drugs, although we still had the Drug B paperwork waiting in the wings should things change. We continued to research, following any updates on the studies, until eventually we realized that we weren't going to need it. We didn't know how long it was going to take, but unless something crazy happened, it felt like she might actually be okay.

January 6

Don on social media

Today is a good day. We were advised that Karen has been on her back for thirty-six hours straight without having to go into a prone position. This shows her lungs are working better. Her oxygen level is at 40. Mary K, a nurse friend of ours, stopped by our house for an update, assuring me that this number is good for Karen at this time. I can't tell you how much that meant to me. The fluid in Karen's lungs has decreased a little. She has not turned the corner yet, but this is a big step toward doing so. I am doing better, but my recovery is a slow process as well.

Thank you for your continued warm thoughts and prayers. Your love is felt.

Kari

During this time, Mom was on a lot of sedatives, so they spent time playing with that mix. They needed to keep her comfortable, turning her prone and supine, and even on her side at times. Mom would try to remove the intubation tube and wouldn't let them hold her down. We discussed our options and decided to put her in large, padded mittens that closed around her wrists with Velcro, then attached the wrists to each side of the bed.

According to the nurses, even though Mom was fully sedated, she was just crazy strong. She could kick her legs really high. I was told mom was really flexible and asked if she did yoga. *Hahaha!* Nope.

Message from April
Today I fed your husband burned chicken and dump-lings. Sorry about that. I don't know what you're thinking while you are lying there. I pray you feel the strength and love of God. I cannot wait until you are home! Love you, friend.

I dreamed I was in a Thai restaurant looking over the menu. Everything was yellow, the tables and chairs and walls, and there was a TV hanging over the counter. Two servers stood behind the counter, talking to each other behind their hands while looking at me. I soon realized that the restaurant was on fire and I was alone. The workers had set the fire and left me there to burn to death.

As I tried to get out of my chair and follow them, I realized that my wrists had been tied to the sides of the table.

In my dream, I panicked. I began pulling and yanking at the restraints as the fire grew hotter. I was terrified. All the while the TV over the counter played the news. The fire somehow extinguished itself, although I still couldn't break free.

Then the news caught my attention as it announced that this restaurant had been on fire, but the patron inside had survived. Meaning me. I worked hard to free myself but remained tied to the table.

Not long afterward, the two servers returned, intent on trying again to restart the fire. They wouldn't release me despite my pleas. Instead, they just left me to burn alive.

Thankfully, the dream changed. I became slightly aware that I was lying in a hospital bed, trying to open the Velcro straps that held my hands to the sides of the bed. I really worked at it, wriggling around, trying to reach the straps with my teeth. I almost got it. I pulled, and the strap began to open. But a nurse looked over, saw what I was doing, and tightened the strap again. Talking to another nurse with her, she said, "She is really smart."

I lay back on my pillow, frustrated.

I dreamed that I had traveled with Ryan to New York City to help him to settle into a new job; he had been hired to do marketing for the Chicken Council of New York (!). The council had provided Ryan with a tiny, dreary apartment upstairs made entirely of oversized Christmas cards loosely sewn together.

Each day, Ryan would diligently create a quirky, imaginative display for the office, and every day they would criticize it and remove it.

After a time, I became concerned that Ryan's spirit was being crushed. My weird reasoning was that if I destroyed the apartment, they'd send us back home.

So, I began kicking at the walls, trying to destroy them. It took a lot of work, but I was successful.

Then the dream ended.

January 7

Don on social media

We are feeling hopeful today. The doctors are starting the long process of weaning her off the ventilator. They turned the pressure down to 10 from 12 and are holding oxygen at 40 percent. They are speculating that damage done to her lungs will be minimal, if any. It is too soon to confirm. They are also trying to give her a "holiday" from her sedation. Kari was talking to the nurse while they were monitoring her, and Momma could hear Kari talking. She reacted to her voice; that was refreshing.

So now we have to be careful what we say when we video chat with her! Karen still has a way to go, but we are ever hoping for a speedy recovery.

January 8

Don on social media:

Good report today. Oxygen down to 35 percent. They are reducing the sedation meds. The doctors are hoping to get her off the ventilator in a couple of days. We spoke to Karen via video chat. She could not talk, but even in her sedated state she was still able the give us a thumbs-up a few times. As for me, this is not going away. I'm still congested. I was told this could hang on a few more weeks. Thanks be to God for His healing. Please continue to pray.

Kari

Mom was weaning off fentanyl. She had been steadily improving, and they were giving her PSV trials, which are spontaneous breathing trials. In these trials, they adjusted the vent settings just to be supportive; they weren't forcing air in, but they let her body take over to see how it works. The idea of PSV is that the ventilator stays in, but they shut off the oxygen to see how her body reacts involuntarily. Happily, Mom was able to go for four hours without support, which is the first step.

The next step was to wake Mom up, which can be difficult since once she woke up, we were asking her to focus on breathing. They wanted her to be able to follow commands, but we were told that patients often want to do well, so they push too hard and breathe too hard. That can be dangerous since they could overextend their lungs or otherwise hurt themselves.

The PVS trials were performed on January 9 and 10, and they decided to take Mom off the ventilator. So, they planned to extubated her on Monday, January 11.

January 10

Don on social media

Drs are encouraged. They are still working to get her off the ventilator. They have performed a few tests, and Karen has responded very well to them. We are all hoping it happens sooner than later. I have been feeling better. The power of prayer is being felt in the Wasoba household.

January 11

Don on social media

KAREN IS OFF THE VENTILATOR!

January 12

Don on social media

Karen had a setback this afternoon. Doctors discovered an air bubble, or pneumothorax, between the lung and chest, and her right lower lung collapsed.

It commonly happens for intubated patients after surgery. It could also just occur randomly.

There was also fluid in her lungs from pneumonia, specifically in her lower right lung.
So, they had to reintubate her.

Kari

They reintubated with a fresh tube and also inserted a chest tube into her lower right lung to drain it of excess fluid and air. The test cultures showed emphysema staph infection in her lungs, which is why she didn't do well when she was extubated. They found a staph infection and MSSA, which is a skin infection. The doctors administered a targeted antibiotic with a fourteen-day course.

Repeated blood cultures consistently came back clean, so the medical staff zeroed in on the chest tube because some days it would remove a lot of fluid and air from her lungs and other days there would be nothing. They finally realized something was wrong with the water seal on the tube, which would pause the suction from Mom's lungs.

Initially, they considered replacing the faulty seal but ultimately didn't need to.

In my next dream, I had just arrived in Sweden. I was picked up at the airport by two very stern women driving a hearse. Since I was supposed to be the guest of honor somewhere, I was insulted to be picked up in a *hearse!*

There was little to no conversation among the three of us as they drove me to the destination. I recall that everything around me was white and sterile. We drove over a bridge and then arrived at what appeared to be a hospital, although I never saw any nurses or staff walking around. I found myself in a nurses' lounge. On a nearby counter stood the framed photo of a nurse, and a posterboard with good-bye messages written on it was pinned to the door.

It had the appearance of a birthday party, but there was no birthday girl.

One by one, nurses began assembling around me. Finally, one of them said, "Our coworker just died, but before she did, she named you to take her place here with us." I was astounded since I'd never met the deceased and had no nurse training. A conveyor belt appeared from nowhere, upon which were the coworker's belongings. As each item passed by, it was placed in a clear plastic bag until the bag was full. Then, as I stood there, they cut a hole in my side and inserted the filled bag in one side until it came out the other side empty. It was very painful, and my last memory was looking at a large clock on the wall and wondering when this would all end.

January 13

Don on social media:

Today is a day of rest for Karen. They just want her to relax while waiting for the excess air and fluid to drain from her lungs.

I am feeling a little better, just tired. Please continue to pray for us.

January 14

Don on social media

Karen has had another day of rest. They had her breathing on her own for a while today. They are trying to strengthen her lungs with some exercises.

I went to the clinic today to deal with my own Covid-19 symptoms. A new chest x-ray showed my lungs are still spotty, so I was given a new antibiotic. I am still feeling weak. It feels like both Karen and I are on the cusp of kicking this thing.

Keep praying.

January 15

Don on social media

Karen is holding her own. The doctors are keeping her in a resting pattern. They are turning off the ventilator several times a day to help strengthen her lungs. The issue is that there are still some infections in her lungs that have been difficult to remove. The next few days will be important for her healing.

I am feeling stronger every day. Still not 100 percent but getting there.

Later the same day from Don

The doctors are patiently waiting for Karen's lungs to get stronger. They are reducing her sedatives to allow her to be more aware of what is going on around her. At this point we are taking it one day at a time. The doctors are encouraged by her progress and have assured us that her slow progress is to be expected.

As for me, I am also getting stronger every day, although I still have shortness of breath but far better than two weeks ago! Please continue to pray for us as we heal.

6

TRANSFER

Kari

Shortly after dealing with the seal on the chest tube, we were notified that Mom was going to be transferred from the cardiothoracic ICU to the medical ICU. She had been in the cardio ICU because they thought she'd require ECMO treatment. She didn't, and they needed the room for a patient being helicoptered in from Arkansas who desperately needed the ECMO treatment. Mom no longer needed to be there.

The medical ICU is the exact same care but with a different specialty.

January 17

Don on social media

Last night the hospital moved Karen to a different room in the ICU. She was moved so a higher-risk patient could have her room. We now have a new care team. They ran tests today and discovered the source of her fever. She has an infection in her lung. They collected a culture sample, put her on antibiotics again, and will target her treatment. The doctors said she is doing well. Still appreciate your prayers and well wishes.

Kari

Mom was transferred to the medical ICU on January 17. At this point, she's been intubated since December 29, 2020.

January 18

Don on social media

The doctors gave us an update: a bronchoscopy revealed some leftover infection from the viral pneumonia, so they are giving Karen targeted antibiotics. Hopefully, we will know soon if there is a chance of getting her off the ventilator sooner rather than later. It is looking pretty positive even with the infection.

January 19

Don on social media

Today is a busy day for Karen. She is being weaned off the sedatives, which is a long process. She is loopy from being on them so long. They are giving her breathing exercises to strengthen her lungs. The infection is getting better. All of that is good; we will find out if her lungs are getting stronger within the next few days. She gets a lot of attention from her care team. We are very grateful for all that they are doing. Evidence of prayer is strong!

Kari

For weeks we had been notified, and even expected, Mom to be removed from the ventilator and given a tracheostomy, which is a procedure that bypasses the esophagus and throat by surgically placing a tube through the neck and directly into the lungs. It also reduces the risk of infection consider-ably.

We expected the procedure to be done sooner, but replacing the chest tube delayed the process. It isn't ideal to have patients intubated longer than a few weeks at most, and Mom has already been on the ventilator for twenty-two days. This was hard on the family psychologically, the waiting and thought of Mom needing a trach. Doctors told us they were waiting to see if they could extubate her, but that wasn't successful.

January 22

Don on social media

Things are an uphill battle, but Karen is responding well. The goal is to remove the ventilator tube next week. She has a couple more days to prepare her body for the tube removal. Her white blood cells are decreasing, and her antibiotic treatment has a few more days. Go away, infection!

This has all been complicated by Karen's sensitivity to medications. Breathing exercises will also continue. It should be a quiet weekend for her. Thanks again for all the love you send our way through prayers and warm wishes.

While at the hospital, Megan came to visit. Apparently, I was a terrible host because I kept falling asleep. At one point she asked if I wanted her to stay, and I nodded. So, she stayed and watched TV with me for a while. I have no memory of this, but it made me happy that I could show my family love even when I was unaware of doing so. Hearing about it later, I was thrilled that she spent that time with me.

Don's latest report

Karen continues to rest and prepare for the removal of her vent tube on Tuesday. As of now her vitals are all good, no problem with her kidneys or liver. Her white blood cell count is down from 12.2 to 8.3, which is in the normal range score of 4 to 10. The infections seem to be under control. She has a fever off and on, which is most likely caused by the sedatives.

As for me, I am strong enough to go back to work. My doctor has given me the all clear. I thank you for all your prayers, we both still need them.

I am also thankful for all of Karen's friends that have provided meals for me. I have about two weeks' worth of food. I have also gained a couple pounds due to the good eats.

January 25

Don on social media

Karen's vent tube is being removed tomorrow! It has been a long, slow course of healing for her to get to this stage. However, there are concerns about the effects of being sedated for so long. So, keep Karen in mind and prayer as she enters this phase of her healing cycle.

Kari

At this point the doctors were doing a lot of monitoring, watching the day-to-day vitals, moment to moment. She was incrementally improving, but it was a roller coaster, what with secondary infections and fevers Mom was experiencing.

The doctors were having trouble finding the source of the fevers. They took blood cultures and ran scans until they had it narrowed down to the sedation itself. Apparently, one sedative she had been receiving had been known to cause fevers. They now are readjusting the sedatives to reduce the fevers while still slowly waking her up. It is just taking time, a lot of time.

January 26

Don on social media

I apologize for getting back to everyone so late, but we did not hear from the hospital until 5:30 p.m.

Karen had her procedure done this afternoon. It went smoothly. The kids and I spent a little time on a video chat with Mama. I'm glad to report that Karen is doing well. Her blood pressure has stabilized since the tracheostomy, which involved taking the vent tube out and inserting a trach tube. They will continue to wean her off the sedation medicine through the night and morning and hope to have it completed in the next few days. The ventilator tube will remain attached to the trachea tube until the weaning is completed. We do not know how long this process will take.

Thanks again for your prayers and positive thoughts. I will let you know what we find out tomorrow.

Kari

This continued through the last half of January

and first half of February. Gareth and I were in constant communication with the hospital nurses and doctors.

At one point the staff would reduce Mom's sedation until she was slightly awake, and then test her responses to commands. They would have her squeeze their fingers, wiggle her toes, and nod (yes) or shake her head (no) to questions. With the trach, she was able to mouth some answers as well. The nurses were really sweet; sometimes they would call us on video chat and say, "She's awake, do you want to see her?" That was awesome!

Then one time they brought her out of sedation, and she didn't respond. She displayed basic responses, such as reacting when someone turned on the lights when they entered the room, but she had stopped responding to commands and this made them nervous. Mom has a history of concussions, which was adding to their concern. She had been responding and now was not.

A PET scan was ordered to test her brain. We were warned that she might possibly have brain damage from being sedated for so long. Happily, she did not, as the scan came back clear.

This is when we first learn about ICU delirium. It's a real thing. Delirium results when the brain experiences the extreme conditions of intensive care; the sensory deprivation caused by isolation, heavy sedation, immobility, and endless days in bed can lead to confusion and paranoia.

Along with sensory deprivation, sensory overload created by intense pain, extended ventilator use, and constant prodding and poking from medical personnel can be a factor in ICU delirium.

One tool that worked for us was the nightly use of video chat. Every evening members of the family, and occasionally friends, would sign on chat to speak, sing, or play music to provide stimulation.

At this point, it had been a whole month in various ICUs, she didn't have a window in her room, and she was looking at the same dull walls every day. This probably contributed to her delirium and confusion. Also, her history of concussions, plus the various sedation meds she was given, made waking up longer and more difficult.

January 30

Don on social media

Karen is doing a little better today. When we called she was resting, so we were unable to do our video chat. They had just given her a sedative to sleep because she had had so much activity. The nurse said Karen could follow her with her eyes, stick out her tongue, and wiggle her toes on command. A real improvement over yesterday. The antibiotics seem to be working, and they wanted to move her chest-draining tube to a lower location. However, due to new arrivals, the ICU couldn't do it today. Weaning completely off sedation could take three days or longer.

I am very thankful for how she's doing; it's encouraging to my heart and to the kids as well. We can't wait till we can see her on a video chat and know that she under-stands us.

February 1

Don reported

Yesterday was a day off from reducing the sedation meds. Instead, they exercised her lungs. She was able to breathe unaided for sixteen hours! Today they continued to reduce her sedation by a small amount.

The ventilator was shut off this morning, and Karen has been breathing on her own. They will continue this until midnight and turn the ventilator on while she sleeps.

She spiked a 102-degree fever, which they were able to treat with Tylenol.

Doctors now conclude that her first round of antibiotics was ended too soon; they are extending this round to two weeks.

February 8

Don's update

Had my first visit with Karen in six weeks. What a visit! When I walked into the room, the nurse told Karen, "Someone is here to visit you." Then I answered, 'Hi, honey!' Her eyes got big, and she put a big smile on her face. Unspeakable love and peace ran through my body! I talked with her for a few minutes, sat with her a few minutes more. Then I got the kids on video chat, which lasted for quite a while. I left a few minutes before visiting hours were over today.

Karen is stable and improving. The recovery is slow,

but she is moving forward. Keep those prayers and warm wishes coming!

Kari
The sedation reduction went on for over a week, but they wanted to be cautious, so they ran trial after trial to see how she responded. During these trials Mom was still on the trach.

Apparently, Ryan came to visit me at the larger hospital. As he watched, the staff attempted to move me from my bed to a chair using a mechanical lift. I don't remember any of this.

For some reason, when the lift got to a certain position, it would lock. The staff tried several times to fix it themselves, until finally they called a technician to repair it. But he was unsuccessful as well. Then someone realized that the strap that secured me in the lift chair was hung up on something, which triggered the automatic stop feature on the chair. Ryan thought the whole situation was funny.

During this time my dreams continued, and they were not pleasant ones. It seems as if I saw the nurses as my enemy; I've learned since then that it's a common theme among patients being weaned off sedatives. Perhaps it's part of ICU delirium.

In any case, I dreamed that I was in a battle of wills with my nurses. Of course, they were winning! I must have had the tracheotomy by then; I kept feeling something tight in the front of my neck. I kept reaching behind my head and pushing forward, hoping to relieve the pressure in the front.

The nurses kept scolding me while pushing my hand away, and I kept saying, "I know, I'm just ..." In what I felt was retaliation, they tied a string tightly around my neck (looking back, it was probably the tie on my hospital gown). I thought, "I can outlast them on this." In my dream, I stayed like this for two days, but that was highly unlikely.

I was also unbelievably thirsty. I remember begging the nurse for more ice chips that she was meting out one at a time. I'd had only a few when she refused to give me more. Again, I felt like I was being punished.

Kari

The doctors informed us that since Mom was improving she no longer needed to be in the ICU and could be transferred to a rehab hospital in St. Charles, about ten minutes from my parents' house.

This rehab facility was geared toward removing the last of the sedatives and adding her usual meds. We were told the average stay was twenty-eight days.

February 9

Don on social media

Today was better than a good day! God's blessings keep flowing! Karen is completely off the IV sedatives. Her days at the ICU are winding down, so we are discussing her future care. She needs a little more time for healing, but a medical rehab facility will be the next course of action.

Kari

We began discussing Mom's transfer to rehab, the timing of which depended on the fever and level of sedation.

In the meantime, she was still not fully conscious or engaging with us, but she was doing well enough to be moved out of the ICU as long as she tested Covid-19 free and had no fever for forty-eight hours.

February 10

Don on social media

Karen is getting stronger every day. This morning they started a 24 PSV breathing exercise/test, and she is doing well. Also, the drainage tube in her lung was removed today.

Our son, Ryan, was able to visit her. She recognized him, although she was still woozy from the sedatives. Tomorrow they are replacing her trach tube with a smaller, more comfortable one. This coming Friday is the target to send her to the rehab facility.

I am thankful for all of you. I am also thankful for the medical staff involved in her care. God has directed their minds, hands, and hearts as they work together to help heal Karen. He is moving in a mighty way.

7

TRANSITIONING TO REHAB

February 11

Don on social media

Karen is at a very hard place in recovery. The physical healing of Covid is underway; the mental part is just beginning.

Earlier today her nurses were talking about their Valentine's Day plans. Karen realized that she had just celebrated Christmas and now it is Valentine's Day. She cried because she lost so much time. That moment was a hard blow to her heart.

As her mind gets stronger, those fears will subside. I am praying for her spiritual, mental, and physical health. We are thankful for your prayers and love as well.

From social media

As Valentine's Day approaches, share your story
***Where you met:** College in Dr. Weeks's class. It was rush week. She sat across the aisle from me. I tried to get her to join our fraternity (men only)*
***First date:** I took her to church and asked her if she wanted to sit up front where the preacher could spit on*

*us. She told me I had a big mouth; I knew then there was
something special about this girl!*

Age difference: *1 year*

Who's older: *me*

Who was interested first: *me*

Who is taller: *me by six inches*

Most impatient: *her*

Who said I love you first: *me*

Most sensitive: *me*

Loudest: *her*

Most stubborn: *her*

Falls asleep first: *her*

Better driver: *her*

Most competitive: *me*

Better morning person: *me*

Funnier: *her*

Best cook: *we both make good dishes.
But she is better.*

February 14

Don's latest update

Karen and I would like to wish you all a Happy Valentine's Day!

*Karen is getting better every time I visit. I brought
her some flowers and a homemade card. She smiled at
the flowers and laughed at the card. She had some pretty
big mood swings while I was there. I noticed that she had
more control over her body movements and better hand-
eye coordination. Weather permitting, she is moving to*

the rehab center tomorrow; snow is predicted in the early morning and expected to last all day.

Karen has a rough road ahead of her as she is entering a new phase of healing. We have been told that the average stay at the rehab facility is twenty-eight days.

February 15

Update from Don

As expected, it snowed all day in St. Louis; about five inches has fallen so far. The city and county are not set up for this.

Karen was expected to move to the rehab center today, but there were no rooms available, so she stayed put. I was told she would be admitted there tomorrow. That's a good thing.

The doctor said that Karen is being "de-ICUed" today. They had her prepared to ship out, so now she's ready for tomorrow. Things are moving forward. Thanks for all your support and prayers.

February 16

Don reported

Today was moving day. Karen arrived at the rehab center between 3 and 4 p.m.

I arrived to visit her at 4:45. Her day was pretty much "move, move, and now adjust." Tomorrow, we hope to get a plan of care.

Karen was more alert. I can see her getting mentally and physically stronger every time I see her. She is now breathing on her own with the aid of oxygen.

NO MORE RESPIRATOR!!

Kari

The doctors at the rehab center began to wean Mom from the sedatives and then slowly reintroduced the medicines she had been taking before she contracted Covid-19, her normal lifestyle medications.

They also planned to remove the trach and get her breathing on her own. After that, work would begin to get her out of bed and walk with the aid of a walker.

February 18

Don on social media

Yesterday was a tough day for Karen. Still adjusting to the new facility and staff. She is still dealing with ICU delirium. Today we have a family video chat meeting with Karen's caregivers. We will be discussing her plan of care and therapy. She has come a long way, with a little bit more to go. Praying for God's Spirit to comfort her and give her peace in her new environment.

When I arrived at the hospital, Karen was sleeping. She only woke up for a few seconds and then slept until I left. Her nurses said she'd been up all night, was a little agitated and confused. Her mind is still scattered from fifty days of sedation. But her body was doing well. They tested her lung strength by capping off the trach and forcing her to breathe normally. Her oxygen level was holding in the high 90s. If she did well in the next day or so, they would consider removing the trach.

Tomorrow Ryan is visiting Mom. I'm hoping that she will be awake for him and that she will have a good night tonight. Thanks again for all your prayers and love that you send our way.

Kari

We knew it would be about a month-long stay at this place, but she ended up doing great and not having to stay that long. After Mom had been at rehab for about ten days, they removed her trach, and she did fine.

Once she had the trach out, she was able to talk very quietly at first, whispering.

Once fully awake, I would insist on wearing my hospital gown backward, mostly because I could remember the sensation of being choked. A nurses' aide would walk in and scold me, saying, "Cover yourself up! We don't want to see all that!"

Standing up after being in bed for over fifty days *hurt!* The muscles in the back of my legs had tightened to the degree I could barely straighten my legs enough to get out of bed. It took two nurses to lift me as I attempted to stand up and sit right back down.

February 22

Don's update

Today was a good day for Karen. Started with physical therapy, which included trying to use a walker.

Right around noon, she got hit out of nowhere with an anxiety attack that lasted for a little over an hour.

She is aware of her physical weakness. It upsets her that she cannot do everything she used to do by herself. Fortunately, she is using that weakness to motivate herself to get better.

I woke up gently. Behind the hospital curtain, I heard the murmur of voices in the room. I appreciated the mattress underneath me that slowly moved to relax my muscles. I was at ease but thought I'd simply had a good nap. Since I'd gone to sleep in a hospital, I wasn't concerned that I'd woke up in a hospital. I didn't realize it wasn't the same one.

A nurse entered my curtained area. Seeing me awake, she greeted me cheerfully. "Hi, Miss Karen. Good to see you're awake."

"How long have I been asleep?"

"Seven weeks."

"Seven weeks?!"

I was in shock. What happened? Now I wasn't so relaxed. I was confused and very agitated. How could I have been asleep for seven weeks? Why couldn't I remember anything?

Now I was worried about where I was. What is this place? Where is my family?

I became more aware of the noise from the other side of the room. Apparently, I had a roommate who wasn't cooperating with the medical staff, and her family was trying to convince her to do so. They were frustrated. I could hear it in their voices.

Two small televisions mounted on the wall across from my bed blared different channels. Machines beeped overhead. Nurses were chattering among themselves. Once they were aware that I was awake, they stopped by to greet me.

Everything seemed to swirl around me. I felt as if I had landed on another planet. Nothing seemed real.

And the beeping! Half awake, I'd hear an obnoxious beeping sound, after which a loud female voice would say, *"Breathe, Miss Karen!"* This would happen repeatedly until

I found myself reaching out, trying to snag whatever that sound was coming from and crushing it with my bare hands.

I imagined that I was at a daycare and someone's toy kept going off. It was difficult to sleep with someone yelling at me to breathe! Ultimately, I learned that an oxygen sensor had been attached to me that would sound off if my oxygen levels got too low.

Don wasn't there at first, but he arrived soon afterward. I was shown an orange silk flower arrangement from Ryan and Megan, and a red Valentine's bouquet from Don. I learned later that the hospital would not allow fresh flowers due to Covid-19 concerns, so Don had to rush home to replace the real flowers with artificial ones.

It seemed as if everyone was overjoyed to see me awake, but I was getting freaked out the more I understood that this had really been a big deal. The loss of time, what I had missed, and trying to understand it all overwhelmed me. Everything seemed foggy, distant.

I was handed a stack of greeting cards that had been waiting for me and realized that I was unable to open them. My hands were numb and useless, the result of not moving for the last seven weeks. They were not wildly painful, simply unusable. Looking at them, I saw that my skin had become a waxy color, almost as if my hands were not human. My legs looked shriveled, and my feet totally freaked me out. I was told by someone later that I now had old-man nursing home toenails!

Don had to open the cards and help me read them. I couldn't stop crying out of gratitude for everyone's thoughtfulness, but also because I felt so lost and confused.

Kari

Mom did have an episode one night where she really freaked out. They called me to ask if I could talk to her to see what she wants. By this time, I was used to reading her lips due to our many video chats.

My dad was in the room, but she wanted to talk to me; I think she thought I could convince the nurses to take out the trach and let her drink water. Or finally have a Diet Coke!

But she was very paranoid. It was clearly the drugs and the panic and being in another new place. All she remembered was that she went into the hospital on December 26, 2020, and now she had woken up after Valentine's Day 2021. So, her paranoia was understandable under the circumstances.

She did kick a nurse, though! She threatened the nurse but was logical enough that when I warned her that she'd have to be restrained, she stopped.

She ended up winning them all over at the rehab hospital. They ended up loving her.

Again, I dreamed about a nurse. This time she was sitting in my room in the dark. I was still restrained.

I'd decided that the restraints were imaginary and that Satan was causing me to believe they were real. I thought if I just rebuked them, they would disappear.

So, I prayed aloud (for the bonds to fall off, but they didn't). I was shocked. The nurse continued to sit across from me in the dark, not moving.

Most of my dreams were gleaned from real experiences

in the hospital. Most of those dreams were of being tortured or mistreated by nurses. But one, even now, makes me laugh.

It seems that as my sedation was being reduced, I became combative and, although restrained, still did quite a bit of kicking. It was difficult at times for the nurses to give me the care I needed because I would turn violent. Case in point, one day it took three nurses to administer a Covid-19 test!

I remember a nurse getting me into some type of headlock and then she said, "You may have the legs, but I have the *finger.*" And then she flicked me on top of the head and left the room. Even in my sleep, I laughed.

Imagine going to sleep and waking up seven weeks later. Imagine going to sleep as one president sits in office and waking up to a totally different president. Or seeing yourself for the first time and your body is shriveled and hands are useless. I couldn't walk, I could barely talk.

Once I got to a mirror, I was horrified at my appearance: my hair was overgrown and somehow stacked on top of my head, my face was strange, and my light gray eyebrows were now dark brown. I didn't recognize myself. I felt like an alien trying to get used to a new body on a strange planet.

There were wires and sensors everywhere. I had sticky pads stuck to my torso with wires attached to them. They'd get disconnected, machines would sound the alarm, and someone would come in to put them back on. This happened so often I didn't even notice when a nurse, male or female, came in to reattach them.

February 21

Don's update

The sedatives seem to be losing their grip on Karen. She is a lot better. The best news is, the tracheotomy tube has been removed. She is breathing normally with the aid of oxygen. She has also begun eating soft foods. We see her getting stronger every day. Nurses had her standing today. I asked her how it went. She said, "Not too good." She will have plenty of opportunity to get stronger.

February 22

Don on social media

Today was a good day for Karen. Started out with physical therapy, which included walking with the aid of a walker. She started eating regular food.

Sometime around noon, she experienced a panic attack that lasted about an hour.

Her hand-eye coordination is improving. She is aware of her physical weakness. It upsets her that she can't do everything she used to do. Fortunately, she is using that weakness to motivate herself.

As I became more aware of my surroundings, I began chatting (whispering, really) with the nurses' aides who would come to check on me or sit with me. Each one would share a bit of their lives and ask my opinion about just about everything from fashion, hairstyles, or relationships. One shared her love of writing poetry, another was excited about an upcoming fashion show, while yet another aide spoke enthusiastically about her love for plants.

Each one would tell me how much they loved their jobs and their coworkers. Hence my early dream about being in a hotel room: these gals *were* having fun!

However, it wasn't all fun there. Not only did I have my physical and mental challenges, but I also had to deal with my environment.

At one point Megan came to visit bearing helpful gifts: two coloring books, a box of glitter crayons, and several magazines. She stayed and chatted until she could see I was getting tired. I loved seeing her.

The room itself was cluttered and noisy; the televisions were never turned off.

My bed had at least four different bed controls, only two of which seemed to work, and I never knew which two they were.

Of course, at that time, I was unable to hold one since my hands were completely numb and my fingers were frozen.

My roommate somehow got the impression that she needed to rescue me, so she'd walk out into the hall and yell that her roommate needed help. Early on, I realized that I was her only roommate, so she must have been referring to *me!*

She had many health issues, was attached to a trach, yet still managed to get up and walk out into the hall, only to have the nurses scurry to get her back into bed and check her stats. I could also hear every … raspy … breath … she took. I felt bad for her, but I felt bad for *me* too! It was very unsettling to hear that sound all day every day. By the end of the day, I'd be sobbing, begging them to move me to a different room. I even told them I'd sleep under a table in the break room! An aide tried to soothe me. She said there was no place to move to. She then bent over me and whispered, "We don't like it either."

They'd have to sedate me at night so I could sleep. During one of my last days there, I said, "Why am I the one who has to be sedated?"

The most memorable situation was when I glanced over at my roommate only to see her sitting on the side of the bed, but she was leaning over on her right side. I feared that she would fall off.

I tried to press the call button, but I couldn't find the one of four that might work. The fact that my hands and fingers were numb and therefore useless didn't help.

Then, I tried calling for a nurse since I was too weak to walk for help.

My voice came out as a raspy whisper. "Hey! Hey!" I tried to call out, but no one could hear me.

Desperate, I looked around to see what was closest to me, which happened to be my walker. I grabbed it and tried to throw it out into the hallway to alert someone. It maybe flew a foot or so, but the clatter finally got the needed attention.

My frustration grew, as I was too frail to motor myself into the bathroom. I had to use a bedpan, which was difficult since I was too weak to do it alone. I was forced to push my call button for help; initially, I was humiliated that I needed help to relieve myself. On top of that, I was so parched, all I wanted was something to drink. At first, it was only ice chips until later when I was approved for juices and water. Then began the unrelenting cycle of liquid-bedpan-liquid-bedpan. Thankfully, I was soon able to wheelchair myself to the bathroom right next to my bed.

The food was good, although I needed some help in eating it. My fingers were frozen open and numb, so holding a fork or spoon was a disaster. I needed help feeding myself and then cleaning myself off afterward. I was a mess.

Slowly, I was able to use a wheelchair and then a walker by myself. I wasn't very good at it, but at least I could get around a little. My first shower (sitting in a chair) was heaven! I discovered that I couldn't raise my arms above my waist; it would take several months and lots of hard work to regain that range of motion.

8

REHAB #2

It was disheartening to learn that I was not going home after my stint at rehab. I was being transferred to yet another rehab facility—housed within the same hospital where I was first admitted. However, it was not affiliated with that hospital.

Talk about going full circle! Here is where my Covid journey began, and now it would end in the same place.

On that day, even though I could sit and stand without aid, I was transferred to my second rehab by ambulance. As I crawled up on the gurney and began the last leg of my journey, many nurses and nurses' aides gathered around to applaud and wish me good luck. I felt like was on a parade float.

As a parting comment, I said, "Now you can use my bed for someone else," to which a nurse replied, "I'm glad you're doing well; the patient who had the bed before you died."

It was the first time I remembered riding in an ambulance. I'd already been transported twice, but of course, at that time I was sedated and intubated.

I have watched many television shows and movies depicting ambulances, but I never realized how cramped they are inside. Plus, the patient is loaded in headfirst, riding forward but facing backward. By the time we arrived at the rehab, I felt pretty motion sick.

While the room at the first rehab was cluttered and noisy,

my room here was huge and clutter free. Apparently, it had once served as a birthing room for the hospital. Now, it was a private rehabilitation suite. And delightfully quiet. Almost too quiet. I was transported in the afternoon, so evening arrived quickly. I had yet to see or hear anyone besides a nurse or someone walking quickly down the hall in high heels. Why do they always wear high heels?

I got a little spooked, so I opened my door so I didn't feel as isolated. I discovered that the bed I was now on was set with an alarm that would sound if I got up. That was fine, I wasn't moving around much anyway.

I learned how loud the alarm was later that evening when I accidentally dropped my iPad off the side of the bed so that it was dangling by its cord between the mattress and the bed rail.

Thinking I could just grab it, I reached down, only to get my arm stuck in that small space. My iPad then disconnected from the cord, so it fell on the floor; I was now stuck between the mattress and the bedrail, unable to remove my arm.

Then the bed alarm went off.

I just dropped my head in defeat as I waited for rescue, knowing I probably wasn't making a very good first impression on the staff.

My room was huge, with space for at least another bed. I had a bathroom to myself, plus there was a huge picture window overlooking the hospital roof and a few roads.

That's when it hit me: on the other side of that roof, over another big building, was *my house!* The house Don and I had lived in for over thirty years, where we raised our kids, was less than a mile away. I'd been away for nine weeks by this time, and I suddenly became very, very homesick.

I also missed our dog, Teddy, our fluffy Labrador mutt,

to the point where it became an obsession. He was all I could think about, besides the fact that I could crawl to my house if I wanted to.

The night nurse was this older man named David who was very professional as he took my vitals and dispensed my meds. I asked him how many patients there were since it was so quiet. He looked at me. "Twenty-six … and I like it quiet." Creepy.

After all the clamor at the first rehab center, I liked quiet, too. Most of the time I would sit in my room with the door ajar, no lights, no TV. The only time I'd have the TV on was after Don would leave to go home. That was when I felt isolated and alone.

The first full day there, I think I met everyone on the staff at the same time. There was a constant influx of people coming in and out, introducing themselves and explaining their role in my care. It became a joke after a while since this was a common occurrence.

I couldn't wait for Don to show up each day. I was still crying off and on and extremely homesick. I was still trying to make sense of what had happened since December. I was trying to fill in the blanks without having answers.

I looked terrible and felt terrible. I wondered if I'd ever regain my wits.

I had a haphazard daily schedule. The poor kitchen staff would have to rush or delay the meals to accommodate the various rehab schedules; sometimes I'd have breakfast between six and nine, lunch anywhere from ten to twelve, and supper from three to six.

Trying to expedite things, I pushed myself to change my own clothes and practice using the bathroom alone, even though the staff didn't approve. I was getting restless to go home, to get my life back together. I was passing the cognitive and physical tests and doing well using the walker and wheelchair. I even had to pass something called a "swallow test" before I could eat solid food. During that test, a respiratory therapist had to sit with me while I ate lunch. She was checking to see how well I did chewing and swallowing solid food. I passed.

They tested my oxygen levels constantly after realizing that I was overdoing it in physical therapy. It had dropped to 82 at one point. I needed to be 90 or above to progress, so they spent a lot of time teaching me breathing exercises to keep my rate up. Each time I faltered, I would look at them and state, "Let's keep going, I'm highly motivated." In fact, that became my mantra throughout the rest of my rehab: "I'm highly motivated."

At random times, I would be rousted from my room and taken by wheelchair to an area where a group of people was playing games. One time I was forced to participate in a game of cornhole, where I was soundly beaten by a ninety-two-year-old man who appeared to have had a stroke. Ever mature, I insisted that I be returned to my room immediately.

I could only have one visitor a day, from 2 p.m. to 6 p.m. Even though I missed my friends so much, I only wanted Don to come visit me. I could tell he was getting overloaded trying to work, visit me, and keep information flowing to friends and family, all the while recovering from Covid-19 pneumonia himself. It wasn't until much later that I realized how much he'd sacrificed for me.

I counted the days until I could go home. It was all I could think about. I tried to keep my suitcase packed and every-thing else within grabbing distance in case I could go home early.

I did have one friend visit besides Don. Stephanie B. had been a friend for years, had been so dear in countless ways. She was my first foray back to my old life. While in the low-est part of my illness, Stephanie prayed for me in the hospital parking lot, helped Don with errands, and served as commu-nicator with other friends. She kept people up to date. I know this was very difficult for her, so I was happy to have her come see me. She couldn't stay long, and I slept for hours after she left.

Other loved ones wanted to stop by, but being allowed one visitor a day, I only wanted Don.

After about a week in that rehab, Don brought me a thick package, telling me it was from my brother, Bob, and his wife, Sally. They wanted to watch me open it via Skype. Once it was open, I saw that it was a beautiful quilt that Sally had made with all my favorite colors. She said, "Everyone should have a quilt when they're in the hospital. The enclosed card read, "More prayers than stitches went into the making of this quilt." From that time on, I snuggled into the quilt at night and showed it off to everyone during the day, repeating, "More prayers than stitches went into this quilt."

As stated earlier, I was so eager to go home, I began counting the days until my two weeks was completed. I was delighted to learn I'd been granted special permission to see Teddy. I was rolled outside in a wheelchair, and Don brought Teddy to me. I could see Teddy's expression brighten as he recognized me. I couldn't get enough of his wagging tail and happy face. As I looked over my shoulder, I could see the nurses' aide wipe away a tear. She was very touched by our reunion. I'd felt good after the visit knowing I'd be seeing him in a few days. What a special treat.

Mentally counting down the days, I knew I was going home on Friday, March 12. Speaking to a clinician, I excitedly told her since it was Wednesday, that I would be going home in two more days.

"Today is Tuesday."

I broke down, realizing I had to wait another day to go home. I was inconsolable the rest of the day, moping around and crying incessantly. Even at the time, I knew I was being ridiculous, but my emotions were raw, and I'd endured so much.

I had hit the wall.

At long last, the day came for me to leave the hospital after eleven total weeks. As the nurse was taking my vitals for the last time, my doctor came in to formally dismiss me. He handed me instructions for aftercare and spoke quickly while I nodded.

Once he left, I turned to the nurse and asked, "What did he say?" The nurse looked at the doctor walking down the hall and responded, "I have no idea."

9

HOME AT LAST!

As I took my first journey out of the hospital, Don and I were greeted by Stephanie, who wanted to record my triumphant exit from the hospital. I felt giddy as I slowly waddled my way out the front door and into the car.

I appreciated every house, car, and streetlight I saw as we drove home. I considered how much living my neighbors had done while I was gone. I was sad but happy to be rejoining them at last.

Driving down our street, I squinted to see our house. Something was there on our lawn, and some people were there, waiting. Michele, April, and Mary had chipped in together to put a large WELCOME HOME sign on our front yard! Our favorite neighbors, Judy, Doug, and Larry, were there to greet me. I was very weak but triumphant as I stood by the sign for pictures. I was home at last!

Thus ended my inpatient hospital experience. Now came the task of yet more physical therapy and trying to regain what Covid-19 had taken from me and my family.

Welcome home

10

ASSESSMENT

Here is the initial assessment of my illness upon entering the hospital:

1. Acute hypoxemic respiratory failure
2. Viral pneumonia with superimposed bacterial infection
3. Covid-19
4. Shock
5. Persistent fever
6. Pneumothorax
7. Encephalopathy
8. Depression, on home Lamictal
9. Hypothyroid, on home Synthroid

Summary upon discharge

You were treated during this long hospital course for Covid, pneumonia, and difficulty to wean from the ventilator. You finished multiple antibiotics courses and will be on a long steroid taper for your lung injury. Our interventional lung doctors placed a tracheostomy to allow you to wean slowly off the ventilator, which they will continue to do at the long-term acute care hospital. You have made significant progress since your admission.

Otherwise, you did need a chest tube during this admission for a pneumothorax (air accumulation around the lungs), but we were able to remove this chest tube after resolution of your pneumothorax.

* * * *

Kari

Mom got to come home on Friday, March 12, but she still needed physical therapy to regain muscle mass and strength. She'd lost nineteen pounds since December 26, so she was very weak, and her Oxygen levels were still low, so we had to track her with a pulse oximeter constantly.

The plan was to attend outpatient therapy at a day institute in St. Charles.

I flew to St. Louis from Los Angeles on Sunday, March 14, to help Mom in her recovery.

I could hardly wait for Kari to arrive! By now, I was more aware of the hard work both she and Gareth had put into helping me survive, Kari with her fervent persistence and Gareth with his dedication and superior communication skills. It made me cry to understand that these two people had put their hearts and souls into my survival.

Seeing Kari walk through our front door, I wanted nothing less than to hold her forever. Our hugs and tears were expressions of pure joy.

Stepping back, I looked into her eyes. I was choked with emotion.

"Kari, I gave you your life, and now you've given me mine."

Her tearful response: "Oh, Mommy."

We all talked and cried and cried some more. It felt as if everyone could relax and enjoy life again.

Immediately, Kari took her post as my nursemaid, telling me what to do, when to take my medications, and when to rest. A firm believer in hydration, she insisted that I always had some water nearby and would scold me if I didn't drink it.

Once home, Kari and I decided it would be nice to send the hospital staff(s) who cared for me a thank-you card with a current picture of me. Along with that we included either cupcakes or cookies from a fancy bakery nearby. Soon we received excited phone calls from various nurses. I'm not sure if it was because of the card, the treats, or the knowledge that someone so close to death had survived.

The picture of me sent to the hospital staff

Gareth had to finish up some work in LA, after which he flew here for a visit. I was so happy. I think he just needed to see me alive with his own two eyes!

11

PANIC ATTACK

I was still quite foggy from the last of the sedatives I still had to take. It never took long for me to drift off to sleep after taking my meds.

However, one evening Kari came to check in on me and I was shaking violently. My pajamas and bedding were soaked, and I was clutching my soggy sheet like it was a gold-filled purse. I was freezing.

Kari was terrified, telling Don she thought I should go to the ER. Don, with his wonderful bedside manner, threw back my covers and pulled the sheets out of my hands, only to take my temperature!

Kari yelled, "Dad, what is *wrong* with you?"

It was time for my next round of meds, so once I'd taken those and had dry bedding, I fell off to sleep. Later, we learned that I had experienced a classic panic attack. Good to know, since I was in no way willing to return to the hospital.

Several days later, I decided that I was ready to get healthy ASAP by pampering myself with a massage. Kari found a place nearby and made the appointment. I bet I gave the masseuse a scare when I came in using a walker, Kari holding me upright. Kari had to help me get undressed and climb onto the massage table. I was ready to get this healing train going!

What a dumb idea.

I thought I was going to die. I hadn't laid on my stomach since I woke up a month earlier. My lungs felt crushed, and they hurt. I felt panic as I started to think I'd survived Covid only to die on the massage table!

I couldn't wait to leave the place and get home. I was disheartened to know I wasn't as far in my healing as I'd thought.

After taking my raft of medicines and being tucked into bed that night, I lay there feeling hopeless. I was sore, tired, and emotional. My hands now ached and my fingers still were unusable. Confusion still enveloped me. I wanted things to make sense and they just didn't. Had someone explained it to me at that point, I wouldn't have understood them anyway.

The following Tuesday, Kari and I attended an intake interview with the local day institute. I wasn't thrilled to see patients in various stages of physical rehab. There were tables set up in one main room, and people were everywhere. One man was pushing himself in a wheelchair while a therapist followed him with a prosthetic leg slung over her shoulder. Some folks were just sitting around, waiting for their turn at therapy. Another person in a wheelchair appeared to have had a stroke. He was leaning severely and never moved.

12

OUTPATIENT REHAB

I wasn't sure I would be able to handle being at this place. Not only was I sick of being in physical rehab, but I saw this place as being an adult daycare and I resented it. But after being hospitalized for eleven weeks, I knew this was the last step before I could put this all behind me. I sure didn't want to go, though. I wish I could say I was a perfect patient, but I was so done with all this, and I really didn't want to be part of it.

In the meeting, I was told I needed physical therapy, speech therapy, and occupational therapy. They wanted me to attend five days a week, but thankfully, my insurance company only allowed for three days, 9:30 a.m. to 3 p.m. with an hour for lunch.

Kari

Mom was exhausted by this idea, but was—I wouldn't say willing to suffer silently—but was willing to do it. She began the next day.

I did not want to go! Everything in me said this was a terrible idea. Kari would get me up in the morning, help me get dressed, and take me to the "daycare."

She would return at lunchtime, having made me a nice lunch, better than I would have made for myself. Then I would sleep in the car until lunch was over. At three she'd return to take me home.

Despite my bad attitude, I appreciated Kari's helping spirit and her unwillingness to let me play hooky. *Nobody* defies Kari! After she returned home to LA, various friends would drive me to and from the center. Thanks, Don, Ann, and Bonnie.

There was a whiteboard at the rehab listing our names and the various times and therapies we needed. I noticed after several days that there would be huge hour-long gaps between sessions with nothing to do. We just sat at these small assigned tables and stared off into space or watched other patients in their rehab.

As I grew more aware, I became restless, asking if I could go do something in between therapies. I was told that I couldn't because they were a daylong rehab, and the insurance company wouldn't pay if we didn't stay on the premises. I was irritated to hear that we had to sit around for over six hours (including lunch), to get three therapy sessions.

Later, I learned that activities were available if you requested them. The staff was very kind and accommodating when they could be. I think they enjoyed my original art, especially the plastic canvas project that spelled out "Yo Mama."

I balked at tracing my hand on construction paper, cutting it out, and making a butterfly out of it. I had to admit later that I wasn't that great at cutting, and my coloring left much to be desired.

Truthfully, it was hard work gaining function in my hands, raising my arms, and trying methods by which I could strengthen my voice. They would have me try to pick up small disks, but I couldn't. In fact, I couldn't even feel them to pick them up. I would just start crying out of frustration. At those times, the therapist would take me back into a quiet room and give me time to calm down. That was helpful, although I realized I was still healing and not at all ready to leave rehab.

I was weaning off various medications, so I began to be more alert, cracking jokes and picking on the therapists. I'd like to think that they enjoyed having me there, but it was tedious. I was counting the days until this would be over.

Believe me, there was no looking back when my time there ended on Wednesday, April 28. Finally, all my rehab was done.

Except it wasn't.

I still had difficulty moving my fingers, my fingertips were still numb, and I still couldn't raise my arms very far. I had to see a physical therapist who specialized in hand therapy. We found Chuck McConnell, who coincidentally knew many of the same people I did, and we would chat while he led me in exercises. We would tease each other once we learned I was one day older than he was. I quickly came to love and respect him as a fellow Christian. He was extremely encouraging, telling me things I needed to hear, whether I wanted him to or not.

During this time, I also saw an ENT for a video stroboscope. The intent was to check my vocal cords to see if there was any lasting damage from being intubated. My voice had improved but was still raspy, getting worse if I talked too much.

Kari

Mom was very anxious about the scope, afraid of

what the ENT would find. She didn't want the trauma of more hospital time or surgery or anesthesia. Test results showed Mom was relying on her secondary vocal cords rather than her main ones, so it became a matter of retraining, relearning, and not pushing so hard.

The first week following Mom's graduation from the day institute was very scary. She couldn't take more than four steps without having to stop and sit down. Using a pulse oximeter, we would wait for her oxygen level to get above 90. If it dropped lower than that, we would've had to go to the hospital. Mom's would drop down to 83, 85, sometimes as low as 79. We'd have to sit her down and get her breathing, oxygenating until she could go again. She was very determined to get stronger.

Her frequent quote was, "I'm highly motivated."

13

MORE HARD WORK

As of today, I have been out of the hospital for over a year. Mentally, I often feel as if I'm still there despite how well I may be doing. Early on, I had dedicated one year to heal and figure out what happened to me and the effect this all had had on my family and friends. Now I see that this will never fit into a tidy little box tied with a bow. It's more like a basket full of puppies: just when you put one into the basket, another one (or two) will pop out. And it will most likely poop on your shoes.

> Text message from April
> *As you get stronger, be kind to yourself and as crabby as you'd like to the rest of us. Except maybe Don and Teddy.*

Four months after being discharged from the hospital, I was able to meet Rammy Yogendra at Kari and Gareth's apartment in LA. He'd wanted to see me while he was there on business, and I certainly wanted to see him and express my gratitude.

We hugged, talking the whole time. Then we sat down and talked about our shared experience.

I'd known about him for years since he'd been friends

with Kari when they both lived in New York. But now I was able to ask him about himself and his medical background. It was as unusual as Rammy himself. I'd heard so many stories about him from Kari. They were so strange they had to be true.

Apparently, both his dad and an aunt were doctors. Rammy's dad is a pulmonologist and critical care doctor who was also a resource for him and our family.

Rammy wasn't always sure he wanted to be a doctor. He first went into public health and then eventually entered medical school.

Rammy and me

I couldn't help but think that this change of heart was no coincidence, that God had directed him years ago to train and be at the right place at the right time.

Rammy told me that during the worst of my illness, he dreaded the possibility of telling Kari that I probably wouldn't survive.

"I know Kari and Gareth were told you had a 5 percent chance of survival, but in reality, it was less than 2 percent. I don't know if it was your family or your faith, but it was a miracle you survived."

I responded, "It was *both*."

14

GATHERING MY THOUGHTS

Since I returned home, I have been ever aware of the emotional toll this experience has cost—not only for me but also for my friends and family. While still in rehab, I began reading the posts Don had faithfully written each evening, keeping everyone updated. I read the responses and the offers of heartfelt prayer. While I was comatose, week after week, he kept up the flow of information while the followers continued to share their love and concern. They were happy when he was happy and encouraging when he was discouraged. Friends Mary and Wendy left gifts of goodies, while there were continual offers of food and offers of help.

There were also flowers aplenty. Real ones this time.

Since awakening from my coma, I have been deeply aware of the thoughtfulness of people close to me and those who I barely knew. I received many cards that expressed high regard and relief that I'd come this far. It was so amazing. I couldn't stop crying as I read each one.

I've noticed the effect a trauma like this has on people, not just for the one experiencing it but also for those who must observe it. Especially that.

It changes you. Makes you wonder what just blindsided you. You tell yourself that the world has righted itself once again. There is an expectation that once a trauma has passed, everything returns to normal.

But there is no normal. Not for anyone.

While I was sedated for eleven weeks, my friends and family had to *watch* me in my struggle to live. I was unaware of the drama going on around me while everyone else waited breathlessly for Don's nightly updates and praying through tears. They must have dreaded checking in sometimes, fearing that *this next post* would be the one telling them it was over. That their prayers were useless. They had to continue their lives, going to work, raising their families, all the while heartsick and praying that I would get better.

I've been told about the inner conflict: should they pray for healing or release? Was it selfish to want me to stay?

As my family and I discussed the possibility of this book, we began sharing our thoughts and feelings about our own experience. Sitting together one evening, with Kari and Gareth on Skype, Ryan and Megan beside us on the couch, each person talked about their individual response to this event. Of course, most of the time I could only listen. It was heartbreaking yet healing to hear just how much effort went into getting me the help I needed.

Ryan didn't tell too many people about his mom having Covid-19. He knew it would be too painful to have to explain what was happening and provide updates to people. As he went about his freelance work as a recording engineer, he had to put aside his worry so he could focus on his job. But sometimes when his work was done, he would walk around his studio yelling at the top of his lungs.

Ryan

I felt helpless, like I wasn't doing anything, and I was angry. Everyone else was being so active with doctors, and sometimes I felt like all that work was just a way to cope with the situation. But I was thinking that to avoid thinking at all. Obviously, I was wrong. I was in denial. I remember the day before Mom was sent to the bigger hospital. It was like a switch flipped when I realized, "Shit, my mom might die." I didn't know if you were going to make it, never really comprehended that it was a possibility until it was laid out on the table.

Kari

I remember getting on the phone with Ryan and Megan during those two crucial days early on where everything was urgent, urgent, urgent, trying to get medicine on New Year's, which was tough.

I remember calling you guys just about every fifteen minutes to run the information past you and asking if we were on the same page. We didn't want to leave anyone out, and I didn't want you to feel like we were dragging you along if you weren't into it. That's when Megan said, "You're not dragging us, we're pushing you."

Ryan

I felt bad that I was the only one who couldn't be involved in everything, that I would have to leave a video chat early because a client was coming from out of town to record with me. I remember feeling like I was disappointing people but also felt there was an unrealistic expectation of what I would be able to do anyway.

Megan

Talking about this brings back my state of mind, which was like panic and terror. It's been hard for me to gather my notes and prepare to talk about this. I'd been keeping detailed notes over the timeline because I was spending every waking moment on it. I would go through six-hour blocks of time and take notes of everything.

Ryan

It seemed like every time there was a video call, I had to cut out early, I had something to do every time. I was sorry if everyone thought I had to prioritize something over this. I didn't want to; that was hard. I felt helpless because you guys were doing stuff and I couldn't.

Kari

That was because we knew Rammy. There wasn't much that you could do.

Me

Kari and Gareth were confident once I was Covid-19 free that you could do the hands-on work that they couldn't do. You and Megan visited me in the hospital, were able to see and touch me, and sat with me even when I was sleeping. They trusted you would let them know if something was wrong or didn't seem right.

Kari

We're definitely never going to forget it. It was very traumatic. On top of everything, I felt so guilty. I was like, "This is all my fault."

My greatest guilt was that I began to think, "It's all my fault that I have taken Ryan's mother away from him."

The trauma was deeply felt by everyone who knew me and my family. Every time the phone would ring, they would fear the worst. Every time a message would post, there was dread that there would be bad news.

As my brother, Bob, noted, "When one of us suffers, we all suffer."

15

MORE PROCESSING

Although I have passed the anniversary of my initial hospitalization, there are still issues I deal with every day.

There is an assumption that once a health crisis is over, life goes on like it was before the illness. That is definitely not the truth.

I was so confused when I woke up. I was greeted warmly by all these nurses and doctors who knew me intimately who I didn't remember at all. I was shown flowers I'd received from family and friends, heartfelt cards that made me cry.

I cried *a lot*.

Over time, I realized that I had just experienced a life-changing event. But so did everyone near and dear to me. While I slept through most of my illness, they were there every moment of every day praying for me, thinking of me, and getting daily updates on social media.

I "slept" for fifty-seven days; they had fifty-seven days of fear, grief, and worry.

I understand that this is a different perspective. It's supposed to be all about me, admitting that they'd just witnessed a near tragedy. However, I've seen how shaky my friends were the first time they saw me at home. Most were happy yet agitated. They had relieved that agitation while helping Don and me during my healing process. As time went on, it was easier for them to share their deepest fears.

Stephanie took a practical approach to the matter, making sure other friends were informed and sharing as much information as she could. I know her heart was breaking. Early in my illness, she parked her car in the hospital parking lot and prayed for me.

My friend Ann hugged me, crying. "I was so worried. I hated that my family could celebrate Christmas as if nothing was wrong while my friend was dying." Ann is not known for emotional outbursts, so this hit me hard, making me understand the fears my loved ones had experienced.

Michele, my rowdy, self-sufficient friend, spent the time focusing on being helpful in any way she could. The Covid-19 restrictions frustrated her desire to take care of Don and me. She went out of her way to give Don vitamins and teach him their uses. Upon our first visit to my home, Michele rushed to me, saying, "I needed you! I didn't know what to do!" Using her large network of friends, she called out for everyone to pray for me, insisting they keep praying.

Bonnie, who is so special to me, couldn't stop crying. In fact, after several months of meeting up for lunch, I finally said, "Stop crying, Bonnie! It's all okay! I'm right here!"

I believe that the isolation brought on by the Covid-19 quarantine led many loved ones to develop PTSD. They were unable to visit, see me, hold my hand, or comfort me. Therefore, their imaginations ran rampant.

My family, of course, had it the worst.

I was allowed one visitor per day for two hours. I was so confused and physically weak that I insisted Don be that visitor. I didn't want to see anyone else for a while. Often, he would leave work, come sit with me for a while, go home, answer texts, and then update everyone on social media. Only then did he have a chance to relax.

Once I was home from the hospital, he waited on me endlessly. I needed it. He had to help me do everything and truly saw my physical weakness. It was hard on him. To this day he teases me about my antics not only in the hospital but once home as well. I know him well; it was his way of processing the situation.

He, and the rest of my family, get angry at thoughtless people who make offhand comments about Covid-19 being fake.

Truthfully, it bothers me to hear someone say, "This too shall pass," or that "God has a plan for you." It's well-meaning, but so shallow and trite to my understanding that I would rather them say nothing at all. To my still-compromised brain, it sounds like I shouldn't be struggling now that I'm back among the living. It makes me wonder how I'm ever going to be able to be an example of what God can do in someone's life. It makes me feel guilty that I'm not on board with that yet.

I also noticed that Covid-19 stories were replacing pregnancy stories. Everyone has or knows someone who's had it worse! If this is a competition, I think I'd rather stay in the locker room.

It was terrible to hear from people who'd lost loved ones due to Covid-19. Here I am, having had a near-fatal case and yet survived, while their loved one had not.

I recognize now that it's important to share with others

what you've been going through, but it is just as important to simply listen when a traumatized person talks about their experience. At this time, the most loving thing you can do is just hear what that person says without comments or suggestions.

16

POST-COVID

Let me share a few of the things I've been experiencing post Covid. Perhaps this relates to you or someone you know as well.

1. **Confusion.** Early on in my recovery, I found it very challenging to understand what had happened during my time under sedation. My response time was delayed so that I answered questions several seconds after being asked. At times I didn't even know I was being spoken to. Everything seemed fuzzy. It was hard to focus on who was talking to me or even how to respond. After a while I would simply start talking in the hopes that something would make sense.

   That blaring TV and noisy roommate certainly didn't help!

   I felt like I owed it to my family to be as upbeat as possible during our limited visits, but I admit I was rarely successful. I still cried and slept a lot. I just couldn't understand very much and didn't respond very well.

   To this day I still find myself confused on occasion. Busy places with lots of people are still overwhelming; I've become sensitive to flashing lights and unending noise. I have fallen in love with quiet.

   When I have lunch with my friend Stephanie, she

takes my money and figures out the tip and how much I need to pay. At this point, I'm using my debit card for most everything, but those ATMs are so confusing, especially since they're all different and have slots and PINs and flashing lights. It's slowly improving; however, if I'm tired and not focusing, it's a lost cause.

The emotional toll is the worst. It's aggravating when trying to have a conversation. I'll realize I'm stuttering and not making sense. That's when I remind myself, "For Pete's sake, Karen. You have a master's degree. Get with it!"

2. **Guilt.** As a rule, I'm not a guilt-ridden person. I believe that every decision I've ever made, whether raising my kids, career choices, or relationships were made through prayer and what I knew to do at the time.

However, one of my first coherent thoughts in the hospital was recognizing the pain my illness brought to everyone in my life. Truthfully, while I was in a coma, my family felt the effects not only for my life but theirs as well.

Imagine having to fear the ringing phone lest it be bad news. I know that Kari and Ryan told very few people about the situation, mostly because they were too focused on helping me. But Don received countless phone calls and texts asking about me and offering to help. Those contacts led him to finally post everything on social media. It was easier to accept unknown friend requests than to continually repeat himself.

I've felt guilty because I'd insisted on going to LA in the first place, despite Kari and Ryan's hesitation. They knew it was too risky, but I'd pulled rank on them. I'm sure part of their trauma is anger that they've had to suffer due to my stubbornness. I can't say I blame them.

This was especially true for Kari and Gareth, as they worked fervently to make sure I got the proper care. They made innumerable phone calls and talked endlessly to medical personnel, all the while having Covid-19 themselves. Not to mention the helplessness Ryan and Megan felt, knowing they were nearby physically, but due to Covid-19 restrictions, they had to stay away.

Added to my guilt is that everyone prayed and agonized over me for over fifty days while I was comatose. At the core of all this, I'm responsible for their pain.

3. **Loss of time.** Imagine reading a book with missing chapters or beginning a movie trilogy halfway through the series. You find yourself trying to figure out the characters and plot throughout the entire story.

Upon learning I'd been "gone" for seven weeks, I couldn't believe it. Where did that time go?

What happened?

I'd gone to the hospital with my reality being one thing, only to wake up in a different world. I woke up to a new president, a new government, and important world events I knew nothing about.

When I'd ask about updates, I was told, "Don't ask."

I didn't really remember Christmas, although there are pictures of us opening gifts. I missed Valentine's Day and Megan and Ryan's birthdays. From that time on, I felt cheated. Spring and summer were upon me prematurely. I'd evidently missed the big snowstorm everyone talked about. It seemed as if I were in a race and all the other runners were several laps ahead and I was struggling to catch up.

While it helped to read Don's posts, along with texts from friends who wrote me during my illness, it still seemed as if I were reading about someone I didn't even know.

It still bothered me to have wasted fifty days sleeping.

And my appearance was shocking. I had been unable to see my reflection while confined to bed. I became aware of how weird my body looked: my legs were shriveled; the skin sagged on my arms; I'd lost twenty pounds. I was told that my weight loss was normal for someone in the hospital. The staff ironically called it "losing the Covid 19."

Most shocking to me, once I got to a mirror, was how haggard I looked. My hair was wrapped wildly around my head as if a furry alpaca had plopped itself there, gotten up, turned around, and plopped down again.

Something else was odd, but for a few days I couldn't figure out what. Then it occurred to me that I suddenly had eyebrows! Dark brown fuzzy eyebrows. To clarify, I've always had very fair eyebrows that I'd never really paid much attention to. Now here they were, seeming like two curved caterpillars over my eyes. Also, my hair had gotten much thinner, which caused me great concern. I was assured that it was the result of an extended fever and was temporary. I'm happy to report that it is almost regrown, plus my eyebrows are back to their lighter state.

It was especially difficult when the anniversary of my hospitalization came around.

I generally enjoy the Christmas holidays, but this

year I thought, "A year ago today I was ..." Frankly, I was a wreck during the entire holiday season as I kept one eye on last year's calendar. Once all the anniversary dates passed, I was able to relax a little.

I still spend a lot of time trying to fill in the blanks of those missing days, even though it can't be done. I have memories of things no one else will understand and vice versa.

4. **Frustration.** It was difficult to accept my limitations once I woke up. I was so weak I needed help to do anything, and it took several staff members to help me.

I couldn't walk at first, so a bedpan was necessary. But my hands were frozen in an open position, so I was unable to use the call button to summon help. Thankfully, the nurses checked in on me often to care for my immediate needs. But oh, how I hated that bedpan!

I couldn't really speak since I had been ventilated for so long. I had to whisper if I wanted or needed anything. My voice has gotten stronger but still gets raspy if I talk too much or for too long. As a matter of fact, I can't really raise my voice to yell at Don anymore! He gets this grin on his face when he knows I'm mad because he thinks my pitiful squeaks are hilarious.

As I mentioned, my hands were stiff, and I couldn't curl my fingers for the longest time. Also, my fingers were numb down to the first knuckle; my physical therapists suspected it was from a pinched nerve in my neck caused by being pronated frequently. I figured it had been more important to keep me breathing than to make sure my pillow was adjusted properly.

I disliked asking for assistance to do anything. I was

a grown woman and should have been able to walk, go to the bathroom, and feed myself without help. Except I couldn't do any of those things. Even trying to put on my own fresh pajamas was painful when I tried to do it by myself.

My expectations for myself were much higher than I could achieve at this point. I had every intention of beating the odds and being back to my old self in record time.

But first I had to learn to maneuver a wheelchair.

That was a challenge because first I needed to be able to get out of bed and into the chair. Before that was possible, I had to get the chair over to the bed and lock the wheels so it wouldn't roll away from me.

It seemed to me that everything was so much work. I was frustrated most of the time initially because my mind had been dormant, and here I was trying to remember procedures for getting from point A to point B.

I don't consider myself to be an overly modest person, yet having a male nurse sometimes was stressful. I specifically remember when a young male nurse asked me if I'd wiped myself after using the toilet. For some reason I felt insulted, saying, "I can't believe you just asked me that." He must have wondered if I knew I was in a hospital for the care he was providing.

Even now I find myself irritated at people, places, and things that I perceive as keeping me from reaching whatever goal I might have for that day. I get frustrated when I compare my abilities before Covid and after. I must remind myself often that I need to trust the advice of my doctors and admonitions of my loved ones to keep working and be patient.

5. **Change in priorities.** Since this incident, I've found that my outlook on life has changed, as have my priorities. I keep replaying the early-morning emergency visit and how I didn't really think it was all that serious. Before, I'd always been sent home once my issue was diagnosed.

   I see now that it could have been my last moments alive, no goodbyes, no loving parting words, no wisdom passed down through notes to my loved ones.

   I was an eyelash distance from death.

   At this point, I don't want to do things just to keep busy. Whatever I do must have value, not only to myself but to others.

   I don't want to contort myself to make people happy. I'm a naturally joyful person, but I want to expend that joy on the people that mean the most to me. After all they've experienced with me, they deserve it.

6. **Isolation.** Of note is my desire to be alone, or with chosen few who can accept me as I am right now. Some of these preferences might be because I was rarely alone in the hospital. While in my first rehab, they even had an assigned staff member sit with me at night while I slept.

   Sometimes I get lonely, remembering how easy it had been in the past to make lunch or activity dates with friends. Now I'm exhausted just thinking about it. If I'm really busy one day, it takes two days to recover. Thankfully, most of my friends understand. In fact, one friend and I have a "never mind clause" in our plans: if either one of us changes our minds at the last minute, we call a "never mind." I appreciate the freedom and I think she does too.

Those last two weeks in the hospital were excruciating, especially knowing my house was only a block away.

I also feel different, unlike anyone else. My near-death experience has made me feel like I'm in a parallel universe, living among people but not being a part of their lives. As mentioned earlier, I prefer being alone, where I can sit back and just think. Not about anything mind-blowing, but rather, just process my experience and pray that one day it will make sense. If it never does, I have to be okay with my new reality.

17

PTSD

There is also the matter of post-traumatic stress disorder (PTSD) resulting from Covid. While I never thought twice about medical procedures, tests, or doctors in the past, I now hesitate to participate even when necessary. I fear anesthesia lest I lose even more time in my life. The last time I took a Covid-19 test, I panicked. I was literally shaking. I'm brought back to that nurse telling me I didn't have the flu. What if I contracted Covid-19 again? I get tested regularly and my antibodies are high, yet the fear remains.

My bad dreams have continued along with night sweats and insomnia. Don reports that I have night terrors on occasion, crying out in my sleep.

I panic if I can't get my arm through my sleeve quick enough or if I can't remove my jewelry by myself, remembering the feeling of the restraints around my neck and wrists.

I'm not sharing these things for sympathy. Rather, it is to normalize these issues if you're experiencing them too. My hope is that you may find some comfort as you compare your experience with mine. Before I even left the hospital, I knew there needed to be something Covid-19 survivors could refer to during the first few months of recovery. Much of our fear was simply because we had no resources concerning what to expect and what was normal in a situation like this. I felt lost and maybe you do too.

I still receive encouragement from my friends and relatives, but the most meaningful to me were the cards I received from Kari and Ryan my first Mother's Day home.

Kari

Mummy!

I can't tell you how full it makes my heart to have you here this Mother's Day. Months back I looked ahead, and when I saw this date on my calendar, I broke down sobbing. The thought that I might not ever get to celebrate you or see you again was, and is, too much to think about. You are my best friend. Thank you for not leaving me.

I love you more than Diet Coke.

Ryan

So happy to spend this and many more Mother's Days with you.

Thank you for not dying.

Ever so slowly, our family humor is returning. We all need it badly to reseed the peace and joy good humor brings. I know I feel tender, as if I'd been through a carwash several times without a car, and my family probably does as well.

As challenging as recovery has been, it hasn't been a completely terrible experience. Along with the bad times, there have been some really uplifting ones. I've always been an optimist. When something went wrong, I believed that bad times made me appreciate the good and I could recognize God's hand in each situation.

If someone would ask why I was upbeat, I would respond, "Every day is heaven because I've already been in hell," referring to my dysfunctional childhood.

Having said that, I can firmly say that I have gained so much from having had such a terrible illness.

This is particularly what I'd like to leave with the reader of this book.

18

LESSONS LEARNED

Even after admitting the struggles during and after Covid-19, I've become increasingly aware of the many great blessings I've received from having had it. After all, most people don't have the luxury of having time to reevaluate their lives and decide if changes must be made.

Now that the window to that insight has been opened for me, here is what I've learned:

1. **Gratitude.** To this day, I don't understand why I survived Covid-19. I most likely never will. However, despite my many questions, I feel a great sense of gratitude for the love and work everyone invested in me. Most days I learn that someone else had been influenced by my illness. Several friends were vaccinated, some worked on self-improvement, and two friends got married. Many people shared that their faith and prayer lives, although tested, grew stronger through this ordeal.

   I've grown very sentimental along with my gratitude. I'm starting to suspect my loved ones are growing tired of my "you're so good to me, I love you so much" comments!

   But I do appreciate things more. Just think of all I might have missed had it gone the other way.

It was a long and painful road, but my tribe walked it willingly. I'm grateful that my family joined forces as a clan coming together to rescue one of their own.

I'm so grateful for my circle of friends who made sure Don was cared for while I was sick. Also, each one created a ripple effect as they shared with their friends, churches, and synagogues and had them pray for me. I'm certain that their combined prayers probably covered the earth many times.

Since Don had kept online updates, there have been people we don't even know following our story. Recently, I saw an acquaintance who I haven't seen for years, shopping with her husband. Her face lit up as she recognized me, and she turned to introduce me to her husband.

"Karen?" he said. "Is this the one who was so sick?"

We had never met, yet he was aware of my situation because his wife was invested in my story.

These are examples I'm aware of. Imagine how many more people are in on it and witnessed my subsequent healing. I'm grateful for that. I hope it encourages and inspires them.

From the time I was a kid and went through tough times, I would pray to God:

"Lord, I'm not very happy about this. In fact, I hate it. But if in the future it'll help someone else for some reason, I'll go through it."

My Covid-19 experience is proving to be helpful in many ways.

2. **Strength.** Reviewing the time I spent in the hospital and subsequent physical rehabilitation, I'm surprised by the amount of strength I had. Certainly not physical strength, but emotional strength that was replenished daily by reminders that I had quite a talented team of caring people around me.

   Yes, I cried a lot, and it hurt a lot. But for some reason I never thought about giving up. It truly never crossed my mind. As stated earlier, I would say I was "highly motivated." I couldn't give up because I owed it to everyone to not only survive but regain my full health as much as possible. I wanted to show how much I honored their efforts by working hard to rejoin them.

   Even now when negative things face me, I keep pushing through it no matter how much I want to quit.

   I've gained an understanding of just how strong I am. This strength comes from a supernatural God. He reminds me I am worth the fight. Because of that, I can continue fighting even when my human strength is gone.

   In the past, I'd assumed that strong people are that way because they are confident in their own abilities. They have no doubt they will succeed, whatever the circumstances. I couldn't have been more wrong. The strong ones are those who are terrified of the situation but keep going despite it. Now *that's* strength.

3. **Testimony.** To me, a testimony is sharing a personal experience giving credit where credit is due. In Bible college, I knew that if I heard the word "testimony" I was in for a long sermon.

   No one can believe I survived. It was a miracle.

Remember Rammy saying I had less than a 2 percent chance of survival? And how he said it was due to either my faith or my family? I believe it was God first, and then my family.

I'm shamelessly open about sharing my Covid-19 experience with anyone within proximity. I have my still-raspy voice and tracheotomy scar to be a testimonial of it. I recently discovered the scars on my right side where the tubes used to suction my lungs were placed.

My pulmonologist was surprised at my recent checkup. My latest chest x-ray showed the scarring in my lungs is diminishing. I'm surprised yet not surprised.

Many people have shaken their heads in disbelief, calling me a miracle. My response is, "God is good. He brought the right people into my life, using their skills to do the work. And through their talents he healed me."

My testimony, or declaration, has brought me into contact with friends and family who have loved ones in the hospital on ventilators. They ask for advice and comfort, which I freely give. Doors have opened to me to encourage others and guide them in finding possible resources that may help them. They seem relieved that there was someone who could share experiences and give suggestions. As I mentioned earlier, there are little to no resources to help the average person navigate this illness. Therefore, just talking to a survivor can motivate someone to keep going.

This might be in response to the not-so-willing prayer I prayed as a teen, "I'm not happy about this. In fact, I hate it. But if, in the future I can use it to help someone, I will go through it."

4. **Acceptance.** I still can't believe all that has happened since December 26, 2020. Sometimes it seems so distant, while at other times I feel like I'm right back there.

Acceptance can be a tough concept, but I'm learning to accept my journey and the ways of the world around me that had previously gone unnoticed.

Believe me, I still get riled up about certain topics. But I'm accepting that I have a story to tell and I'm living proof of that story. I'm accepting what few limitations I still deal with, such as my voice, PTSD, and low stamina at this point. My hands are usable and I'm very mobile, though wobbly at times.

I accept that "Covid-19 survivor" must now be added to the résumé of my life. My identity has morphed into the truth that miracles do happen. If it encourages someone else, I'm okay with that.

One quick story:

Once home from the hospital, Don waited on me faithfully. He willingly served food he had made and brought me water bottles he'd opened for me because I couldn't do it myself. After a few weeks, he handed me an unopened can of soda, intending to pull the tab on it himself. I took the can, grabbed the tab, and slowly opened it myself.

Don just stood there. I thought he was kidding when he said, "You opened it yourself!" I soon realized he was serious when I overheard him on the phone with his family: "Karen just opened a can of soda by herself!"

5. **Joy.** Even before I contracted Covid-19, I believed God had gifted me with joy. It was an attribute I appreciated even in down times.

Once I woke up, joy was hard to find. I was too confused to recognize much of anything. But once my mind cleared and I could interpret what had happened, I found joy in little things (except the bedpan). I felt joy when I could get out of bed, when I could take a shower, and when I could feed myself using a real utensil. I felt joy when able to brush my own teeth and change my own clothes. It was joyful to visit with the nurse as if we were old friends, and I'm sure they were relieved to see I wasn't really an uncooperative patient!

Extreme joy filled me when I saw Don in person, when Megan and Ryan came to visit, when Kari and Gareth came to see me at home, and when I received all the love everyone had been holding onto for so long. We all laughed with giddy happiness and cried with great relief.

6. **Faith.** "Faith" is an easy word to throw around when you can't think of anything else to say. Have faith. I have faith in you. Have faith in yourself. Have faith in God. For me, I replace the word "faith" with "confidence." Confidence that God will do what he says he will do. Confidence that he is aware of our struggles and will guide us through them.

I believe faith/confidence is the only thing you can rely on when nothing else works. A great deal of my faith came from putting pieces together from my hospital experience. Most of the things that helped me don't happen very often. Realizing that, my faith increased once I saw his hand in it all.

While doing all my rehab, I repeated, "God will get me past this. Look what he's already done." Sometimes that belief was all I had to cling to during those rough days. Also, for me, faith implied persistence and stubbornness, knowing that God would do what he said he would do.

My Covid-19 experience also stimulated the faith of those who witnessed it. How else could you explain the miracle of my healing? Seeing prayers really work gave people energy and peace and made God even more real. I asked some friends what their biggest lesson from this experience was. Every one of them said their prayer lives improved, and along with that, their faith had grown stronger.

19

NO COINCIDENCES

I don't believe in coincidences. Everything that happened to me demonstrated a deliberate move to have the right people in the right place at the right time.

- Rammy "just happened" to become a doctor despite his parent's disapproval.
- Rammy "just happened" to gain a deep interest in Covid research, subsequently networking with other Covid researchers.
- Kari and Gareth "just happened" to meet Rammy in New York, Kari joining the band Rammy was in while he was still in med school, and continued their friendship over the years.
- Rammy's dad "just happened" to be a medical doctor who also had an interest in Covid. Remember, he affirmed to Rammy that Don did indeed have Covid-19 pneumonia and used resources to help him.
- Through Kari and Gareth's persistence in getting the FDA approval for Drug B (which we never needed), many notable researchers "just happened" to get involved, which drove them to rewrite the protocol to include more patients. Because of this, more Covid-19 patients at least had the option to apply for and

potentially use experimental medicines to aid in their healing. Perhaps more patients survived because of that work.

- It "just happened" that despite the demand for inpatient care, there was always that one last bed available for me.

- When in my three different rehab facilities, most therapists "just happened" to know other therapists, so I received uninterrupted care as everyone followed up on what I needed. On top of that, two therapists from two separate facilities were a married couple who created a bond that encouraged me to be diligent in rehab.

- When doing my final rehab for my hands, I "just happened" to be referred to a wonderful physical therapist who brought much-needed encouragement to me. Chuck not only helped with my therapy but strongly encouraged me to write this book. The fact that he "just happened" to know many of the same people I did, convinced me that our meeting was not a coincidence.

I noticed just recently that my life has been divided into "BC" and "AC," before Covid and after Covid. When someone describes an event or incident, I immediately categorize whether it happened before my illness or after it. There is regret for the time lost, but I'm learning to surrender that regret.

20

FINALLY

Many people believe that God causes things to occur to test us, or even punish us. I bet some people wondered what I had done to deserve Covid-19. I don't believe I did anything to deserve it. Some things just happen. We live in a world with good and evil, sickness and health.

However, I do feel that it's up to us during those bad times to turn to God. He's right here to access.

Over a year after my illness and recovery, people are still referring to the miracles that occurred. Some get emotional as they relate their fear and ultimate relief that it turned out well.

It seems as if my Covid-19 experience opened the hearts of those who just needed assurance that life wasn't always unfair. They look at my healing with hope and maybe the willingness to believe again.

Through my story you can begin to have hope again. My aim in sharing my experience is to let you in on what happened to me. Perhaps you or a loved one has a similar story even more dramatic than mine. So little was known about Covid-19 in its infancy that no one—not medical personnel, not politicians, not even the health organizations—had a definitive solution to cure it.

That left a lot of people scared, isolated, and confused. We lost our compass and didn't know where to turn.

I truly believe that God didn't cause this but that he's leading us to seek him for guidance, wisdom, comfort, and strength. There has been a change not only in me but also in the circle of people in my life. Family has become more important, as have close relationships. There has been more of an effort to spend real time with people I care about. I've seen evidence of an increased willingness to communicate both on a physical and spiritual level.

This change is not due to me personally; rather, it serves as a real lesson about how fragile life is. One minute I was fine and the next minute I just … wasn't.

Not many get to witness a real-life miracle, and to be honest, most people won't in their lifetime.

But those who have been privy to my near-death experience have the opportunity, through my ordeal and healing, to examine their own lives as I thank God for mine.

I want you to know that you are not alone in your post-Covid journey. Your emotions, reasoning ability, and physical attributes have all been short-circuited, and it will take time for things to be put back together. Some things may not improve. My voice will likely stay this way, and my need for quiet may be permanent.

However, this can make new benefits possible: Don enjoys not being able to hear me when I speak, and I've had the quiet needed to write this book.

May my story not only instruct you but also comfort and inspire you. Know that your distresses do not have to destroy you. There is a mighty God who not only shows His face in an obvious way but who also works behind the scenes in ways you may never discover.

There is no such thing as a coincidence.

As you remember your community of friends and loved ones, keep moving forward, and never give up your hope for a meaningful outcome in your life.

Go easy on yourself. Your body may be impaired, but your spirit will never be.

Hang in there. Observe the positives and accept the negatives brought into your life through the experience of Covid.

Become highly motivated to really inhabit more of your life. Rest if you need to, sleep if you need to, pray because you must. You and your loved ones aren't alone in this experience.

I hope that this book will encourage you and validate what has happened or is happening in your life regarding Covid-19.

May God bless you and bring you peace.

My family: (left to right)
Ryan, Megan, Gareth, Kari, Don, and Karen